BREAD & BEYOND

Original Bread Recipes for Every Occasion

BEVERLEY SUTHERLAND SMITH

ORBIS · LONDON

CONTENTS

First published in Australia 1985 by Bird's
Country Mill Pty Ltd. (Inc. in Victoria)
This edition published in Great Britain 1986
by Orbis Book Publishing Corporation Ltd.
A BPCC plc company
Greater London House, Hampstead Road,
London NW1

© Beverley Sutherland Smith, 1985
Photography: Bunge (Australia) Pty Ltd.

Printed in Italy

British Library Cataloguing in Publication
Data
Smith, Beverley Sutherland
   Bread and beyond: original bread
   recipes for every occasion.
   1. Bread   2. Yeast   3. Cookery
   I. Title
   641.8'15   TX769

ISBN 1-85155-000-3

INTRODUCTION

One of the most satisfying of all foods, bread has traditionally been called the 'staff of life'. The baking of bread can be traced back 5000 years to the times of ancient Egypt, where it was made in shapes to resemble a sphinx or pyramid, braided, or formed into circles.

In medieval times, bakers were highly regarded members of the community and in many countries bread was considered such an important staple that bakers were governed by complicated laws. The punishment was severe for crimes such as over-pricing and this was carefully monitored, as was the selling of bread made with inferior or bad flour. In England the baker was usually placed in a pillory but sometimes tied to a sledge and drawn through the town, the faulty loaf tied around his neck to deter others.

Nowadays there are few small local bakers, as large commercial companies have taken over the marketing of bread, delivering it to shops and supermarkets hygienically sealed and brightly packaged. It has good keeping qualities but too often lacks flavour and texture.

As there has been a return to natural things and natural foods, so has there been a revival and interest in making bread at home. There is a special satisfaction in kneading the dough and watching it rise gently, and there is no aroma in the world that stirs the senses and warms a house like that of a loaf of bread baking in the oven. Home-made bread has a special charm with the slight irregularities of its appearance and a flavour and texture that are quite different from the commercial product.

Many people have reservations about making bread, and are often deterred by the belief that it is difficult, tedious and time consuming. It does take time for the yeast to begin to work and the dough to rise, but you can be doing something else in the meantime. The availability of strong (bread) flour, suitable for baking, and very

stable yeasts has made baking bread at home much easier. If you do not want to spend time and energy on the physical effort of kneading the dough by hand, an electric mixer and a dough hook give equally good results.

In all the recipes in this book the quantity given is for dried (active dry) yeast. Fresh (compressed) yeast can be easily substituted if available, in the following proportions: 8 g dried = 15 g/ ½ oz fresh yeast; 12 g dried = 25 g/ ¾ oz fresh; 16 g dried = 30 g/1 oz fresh.

Bread freezes excellently, so take advantage of this when making a large quantity of a basic bread dough. As fancy breads are at their best eaten within a day or two, the recipes given here are usually for one loaf.

Bake bread regularly and you will soon find that there is much more to it than loaves, buns or rolls. For example, it takes little more effort to make a meat pie with bread dough rather than pastry, and the result is far more economical and satisfying for a family, and can be kept for a longer period of time. Basic bread dough can be filled with bacon, eggs or cheese, used as a base for a quiche or rolled around sausages; the variations are infinite.

The more often you make bread at home, the more confidence you develop and the easier it becomes, but half the fun is that, even for the most experienced, no two loaves are ever exactly the same. The final result is a matter of your own personal preference; you may like a very crunchy crust and choose to leave the bread a little longer in the oven, or perhaps your preference is for a close-textured or particularly moist loaf.

Handling yeast, baking breads and developing your own ideas is an adventure in cooking and provides pleasure for the whole family, whether it is just enjoying the results, or sharing in the making.

Beverley Sutherland Smith

Basic Bread-Making Techniques

KNEADING

Kneading is one of the most important stages of making bread because it develops the gluten which gives the dough its elasticity, and distributes the yeast evenly. You should not need to use extra flour when handling your dough if the correct amount of liquid has been used, but as flour and conditions vary, always use your own judgment when kneading the dough as to whether a little more liquid or a little more flour may be required. It is easier to have the dough on the moist side to begin with and knead in a little extra flour, than to have a dry, hard mixture.

To knead by hand, take the edge of the dough and pull it into the centre with your fingers. Push out again with the heel of your hand so that the dough rolls on the board. Then give the dough a quarter turn and repeat. Knead for seven to ten minutes.

To test if the dough is sufficiently kneaded, lightly push a finger into the mixture. If it springs back it is ready. Electric mixers with a dough hook give good results and save some time and a good deal of energy. If ingredients such as seedless raisins or nuts are to be added, it is best to knead the dough first, then mix these in by hand.

PROVING

To prove dough, place it in a warm, draught-free place. The warmth will cause the dough to rise. It will rise even in cool conditions, but takes much longer.
Here are some places to prove your bread:
- Near an open fire, heater or a heating duct.
- In a sheltered sunny position, such as a window sill.
- In the warming drawer of a stove.
- On a wire rack placed over a food warmer.
- On an electric frying pan with a wire rack placed on it.
- In a shallow baking tin or dish half filled with very hot water.

The dough should be warm, but be sure you do not allow the bowl or loaf pans to become too hot.

Wholemeal (whole wheat) and grain doughs take longer to prove, as they are heavier in texture.

Rely on the look of the dough – it should double in size – rather than judging by time. To test, press lightly with your fingertips; the indentations will remain when the dough is fully risen and ready for baking.

COOKING & STORAGE

Bread should be baked in a very hot oven so that the yeast is killed quickly by heat and the dough does not continue to rise. For most plain breads the oven temperature remains the same throughout baking, but you will notice that some fancy breads require the oven temperature to be altered so they cook more evenly. If the bread or buns are browning too quickly on top, cover them loosely with foil.

When cooked, bread should sound hollow when tapped on the base and sides. If it is not ready, invert the loaf and return to the oven for another five minutes or so. For a firm, crisp crust, cool the bread on a wire rack.

Store the bread in a bread crock or in a plastic bag in a cool pantry. Most breads, with the exception of some rich fruit breads, do not benefit from refrigeration, unless the weather is particularly hot. Once cool, the bread can be frozen for up to two months. Leave to thaw at room temperature and crisp the crust again by placing in a hot oven for about ten minutes.

DIRECTIONS

TALL LOAVES

1 kg/2 lb of basic dough makes two large loaves, each 750 g/1½ lb in size. The basic white or wholemeal (whole wheat) bread will be taller and slightly larger than the whole grain or rye bread which has a denser texture and makes a smaller loaf.

Leave the dough to prove until doubled and divide into four equal portions. Working with one portion at a time, punch the dough down to flatten and remove the air. Roll up firmly and turn seam side up. Repeat with the other portions. Pinch the ends and place two portions of dough, seam side down, in each greased loaf pan. Cover pans with greased or oiled cling film (plastic wrap) and leave to prove until doubled. White or wholemeal (whole wheat) dough will prove more quickly than grain or rye.

Remove the covering, and glaze the top gently either with egg beaten with a couple of teaspoons of warm water, or warm water. Sprinkle with seeds or scatter some flour over the top. Bake in centre of a preheated hot oven, 230°C/450°F, gas 8 for about 12 to 15 minutes.

ROUND BREAD ROLLS

To make bread rolls, prepare one of the basic breads, either white, wholemeal (whole wheat), rye or seed and grain. 1 kg/2 lb of dough makes 32 rolls.

When the dough has proved until double in size remove from the bowl and divide into four. Each quarter will make eight rolls. Make the eight sections as even as possible. Press each portion with the palm of your hand to expel air and shape by cupping the palm of your hand and rotating it continuously until the dough gathers into a round ball.

Place on a greased baking tray (cookie sheet) with the puckered part underneath. Cover with greased oiled cling film (plastic wrap) and leave to double. Glaze if desired with egg beaten with water.

Bake in centre of a hot oven, 230°C/450°F, gas 8 for about 12 to 15 minutes.

KNOT ROLLS

Divide the dough into equal portions as for Round Rolls.

Roll each piece into a thin sausage, about 20 cm/8 in long, and tie into a knot. Cover and prove until double in size and bake at 230°C/450°F, gas 8 for 12 to 15 minutes in the centre of the oven.

FRENCH BREAD STICKS

1 kg/2 lb of dough makes four French sticks. The basic white or wholemeal (whole wheat) dough is more suitable for a French bread stick than the heavier seed and grain or rye.

Leave the dough to prove until doubled. Punch down and divide into equal quarters. Using a quarter of the dough, roll up firmly. Place two hands on top and gently elongate the dough by rolling to about 30 cm/12 in in length. Place on greased baking trays (cookie sheets) or in traditional French bread stick tins. Repeat with remaining portions of dough. Cover with greased cling film (plastic wrap) and prove until doubled. Remove covering.

Slash with a razor blade and glaze gently with beaten egg or warm water. Sprinkle with seeds, oats, rock salt or flour. Place tray in centre of a preheated hot oven, 220°C/425°F, gas 7 and bake for about 25 minutes.

FREE-FORM LOAVES

A free-form loaf is the term used to describe a loaf cooked on a flat baking tray (cookie sheet). Some examples are cob loaf, log loaf, plait, and cottage loaf.

COB LOAF

1 kg/2 lb of dough makes three cob loaves.

When the dough has proved for the first time, take one third and knock down to remove air. Pat into a smooth round. Place on a greased baking tray (cookie sheet) and cover with greased cling film (plastic wrap). Repeat with remaining portions of dough. Leave until doubled and remove covering.

With a razor blade make two shallow slashes across the top of the loaf to form a cross. To make the top extra crusty, slash the dough more deeply.

Glaze with beaten egg or warm water and sprinkle with seeds or flour. Bake in centre of a preheated hot oven, 220°C/425°F, gas 7 for about 25 to 30 minutes.

COTTAGE LOAF

1 kg/2 lb of basic dough makes two cottage loaves.

When the dough has doubled for the first time, knock down to remove air. Divide in half, then divide each piece into two, one twice the size of the other. Pat the larger piece into a smooth round and the smaller piece into the shape of a tear drop. Place the larger piece on a greased baking tray (cookie sheet), press two fingers straight through the centre and place the tear drop shape into the hole. Cover with greased cling film (plastic wrap).

Repeat with the other piece of dough and prove until doubled in size. When doubled, remove covering.

Glaze with beaten egg or warm water and sprinkle with seeds or flour. Bake in centre of a preheated hot oven, 220°C/425°F, gas 7 for about 30 minutes.

PLAIT

1 kg/2 lb of dough makes three plaits.

When the dough has proved for the first time, divide into three portions. Knock down one of these to remove air and divide this into three equal portions. Roll each one into a smooth sausage shape and lay side by side, pinching top ends together, and plait. This is done by working from right to left, laying the first piece over the next one and under the third. Repeat until the plait is complete, pinching the ends together. For a neater finish, tuck the ends under.

Repeat process for remaining portions of dough. Place on a greased baking tray (cookie sheet) and cover with greased cling film (plastic wrap). Prove in a warm place until doubled.

Remove covering, glaze with beaten egg or warm water and sprinkle with seeds or flour. Place tray in centre of a preheated hot oven, 220°C/425°F, gas 7 and bake for about 25 to 30 minutes.

LOG LOAF

1 kg/2 lb of bread dough makes three log loaves.

Prepare the dough and leave until doubled. Take one third and knock down to remove air. Flatten into a rectangle and roll up firmly to make a log shape. Pinch ends together and place seam side down on a greased baking tray (cookie sheet). Repeat with the other two pieces. Cover with greased cling film (plastic wrap) and prove until doubled. Remove covering and with a razor blade make three diagonal slashes across each loaf.

Glaze with beaten egg or warm water and sprinkle with seeds or flour. Bake in centre of a preheated hot oven, 220°C/425°F, gas 7 for about 25 to 30 minutes.

WHITE BREAD

WHITE BREAD

This simple loaf has a crisp crust, fine texture and excellent flavour. Very good fresh or toasted, it forms the basis of many of the more unusual ideas in this book. Use it as the crust for a quiche or pie; vary it by adding fruits, vegetables or nuts to the dough.

The ingredients are flour, yeast, salt, water and a little sugar; nothing could be simpler. If you are not confident about making bread, this is a very good loaf to begin with. Use a strong (all-purpose) flour, the kind sold especially for making bread, rather than the softer cake flour. The amount of salt added is a matter of

personal taste, but remember that bread without any has little flavour. A small quantity of butter or margarine – 30 g/1 oz (2 tbsp) mixed with the flour to a crumbly texture – enriches the bread; Milk Bread (page 20) and Egg Bread (page 24) are other examples of enriched breads.

Keep the crust plain, give it a light dusting of flour or glaze it with water and top with poppy, caraway or sesame seeds. Slash the top of a free-form loaf to make a pattern and glaze with beaten egg; do this just before baking or the pattern will disappear.

The following quantity makes two large loaves, each 750 g/1½ lb, about 30 to 36 bread rolls or four French bread sticks.

Metric/Imperial	Ingredients	American
16 g/4 tsp	Dried (active dry) yeast	4 tsp
1 tsp	Sugar	1 tsp
570 ml/19 fl oz	Warm water	2⅓ cups
1 kg/2 lb	Strong white (all-purpose) flour	8 cups
3 tsp	Salt	3 tsp

Place the yeast, sugar and warm water in a bowl and stir. Leave to stand for about ten minutes or until some froth has formed on top. Sift the flour and salt into a bowl, make a well in the centre and add the yeast liquid. Mix to a dough. Knead by hand (or in an electric mixer using a dough hook) for seven to ten minutes. If still sticky after the first few minutes, add a little flour and knead into the dough; if dry, add a spoonful of warm water. When elastic, cover with greased or oiled cling film (plastic wrap). Leave in a warm place for about an hour or until doubled in size.

Punch down the dough. Form into two large loaves, rolls or bread sticks or any combination of these. Place the dough in greased loaf pans, or if making free-form loaves, on a greased flat baking tray (cookie sheet). Cover again and leave in a warm place for about 45 minutes to an hour to double in size.

Bake in the centre of a preheated hot oven, 220°C/425°F, gas 7 for 25 to 30 minutes for large loaves, 12 minutes for bread rolls and about 15 to 20 minutes for bread sticks. The base and sides of the bread should sound hollow when tapped. Leave to cool on a wire rack for a crisp crust.

BACON AND ONION FILLED ROLLS

These little bacon and onion rolls are inspired by pirozhki, which are tiny Russian pasties (turnovers) made with a yeast dough, containing all types of interesting fillings such as minced beef, veal, chicken, mushrooms, or sometimes cheese. Served piping hot and eaten with soup, they make a substantial beginning to a meal. Although, as in Russia, they are wonderful to serve with soups, they can also be eaten on their own as a snack, an appetizer or to accompany a dish such as a plain omelette, salads or vegetable dishes.

Pirozhki reheat particularly well. Cover lightly with foil and warm in a moderate oven for about five to eight minutes, depending on whether they are a day or more old. They freeze very well and can be reheated after thawing.

Place the yeast, sugar and water in a bowl and stir. Leave to stand for about ten minutes or until some froth has formed on top. Sift the flour and salt into a bowl. Make a well in the centre, add the yeast liquid and mix to a dough. Knead by hand (or in an electric mixer with a dough hook) for seven to ten minutes. Cover with greased cling film (plastic wrap) and leave in a warm place for about an hour until doubled in size.

Place the bacon in a dry frying pan and cook until the fat is transparent and bacon slightly crisp. Remove and drain, leaving the fat in the pan. Add the onion to this and cook, stirring occasionally over gentle heat until the onion is transparent and softened. If there is not sufficient fat, you can add a little oil. Remove the onion and mix with the bacon. Season generously with pepper; don't use salt as the bacon will supply plenty. Cool.

Punch down the dough and form into a circle. Roll out with a rolling pin to a thin layer. Cut out circles about 8 cm/3 in in size. Remove each circle, then roll it again so it is a little thinner and larger.

Place about a teaspoon of filling on one side of each circle, fold over and press the edges together firmly to seal. (Gather up the scraps and roll out again.) Place on a greased baking tray (cookie sheet) and cover with greased or oiled cling film (plastic wrap). Leave in a warm place for about 25 to 30 minutes or until doubled.

Before baking check the edges again to see if they are still sealed. Beat the egg with water and brush the tops and seams with the glaze. Scatter a few sesame seeds on top. Bake in a hot oven, 220°C/425°F, gas 7 for about ten minutes.

Metric/Imperial	Ingredients	American
8 g/2 tsp	Dried (active dry) yeast	2 tsp
1 tsp	Sugar	1 tsp
285 ml/9 fl oz	Warm water	1 cup + 2 tbsp
500 g/1 lb	Strong white (all-purpose) flour	4 cups
1 tsp	Salt	1 tsp
250 g/8 oz	Bacon slices, diced	8
1	Large white onion, finely diced	1
	Black pepper	
	Glaze	
1	Small egg	1
2 tsp	Water	2 tsp
	Sesame seeds	

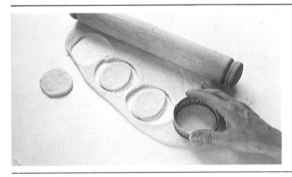

Bacon and onion filled rolls ▷

BREAD ROLLS WITH FRANKFURTERS

Hot dogs are nowadays a popular fast food, but nothing can compare with the flavour of a continental frankfurter baked at home inside this light, crisp white bread. The bread rolls may be eaten when freshly made but can also be reheated successfully, and will keep for 36 hours if wrapped and stored in a refrigerator. Serve with relish, tomato sauce (ketchup) or mustard.

Metric/Imperial	Ingredients	American
8 g/2 tsp	Dried (active dry) yeast	2 tsp
1 tsp	Sugar	1 tsp
285 ml/9 fl oz	Warm water	1 cup + 2 tbsp
500 g/1 lb	Strong white (all-purpose) flour	4 cups
1½ tsp	Salt	1½ tsp
8	Frankfurter sausages	8

Place the yeast and sugar in a bowl, add the warm water and stir. Leave to stand for about ten minutes or until some froth has formed on top. Sift the flour and salt into a bowl. Make a well in the centre, add the yeast liquid and mix to a dough. Knead by hand (or in an electric mixer with a dough hook) for seven to ten minutes. Cover with a piece of greased or oiled cling film (plastic wrap) and leave in a warm place for about an hour until doubled.

While the dough is proving, place the frankfurters in a saucepan and cover with cold water. Bring to a boil and immediately drain them. When cool enough to handle, remove the skins, which would become tough if baked in the rolls. Divide the dough into eight sections of equal size. Form each one into an oval and roll out. They should be just a little longer than the frankfurters and wide enough to wrap around. Place the frankfurter on each piece of dough. Tuck in the ends and roll over to enclose. Pinch where they join so the dough will not unravel. Place on a greased baking tray (cookie sheet) and leave in a warm place for about 20 minutes or until slightly risen. They should not double in size or the bread will be too thick.

Bake in a hot oven, 230°C/450°F, gas 8 for about 15 minutes. Leave for five minutes before eating.

Reheat in a moderate oven, 190°C/375°F, gas 5 for about seven to eight minutes or until heated right through.

BREAD WITH MACADAMIAS AND COCONUT

Macadamia nuts, first found in Australia, are expensive, but have a unique flavour and texture which combines perfectly with coconut in this special bread.

Serve it with salads, curried or chicken dishes, or with fruit and cheeses for dessert.

If you cannot obtain macadamia nuts, use blanched almonds instead.

Metric/Imperial	Ingredients	American
8 g/2 tsp	Dried (active dry) yeast	2 tsp
1 tsp	Sugar	1 tsp
285 ml/9 fl oz	Warm water	1 cup + 2 tbsp
75 g/2½ oz	Macadamia nuts or blanched almonds	½ cup
45 g/1½ oz	Desiccated (dried shredded) coconut	½ cup
500 g/1 lb	Strong white (all-purpose) flour	4 cups
1½ tsp	Salt	1½ tsp

Place the yeast and sugar in a bowl. Add the warm water and stir. Leave to stand for about ten minutes or until some froth has formed on top. Mix the nuts and coconut together. Sift the flour and salt into a bowl, make a well in the centre and add the yeast liquid, nuts and coconut and mix to a dough. Knead by hand (or in an electric mixer using a dough hook) for seven to ten minutes. Cover with greased or oiled cling film (plastic wrap) and leave in a warm place for about an hour until doubled.

Punch down and form into two balls. Place them in a 750 g/1½ lb greased loaf pan. Cover with greased or oiled cling film (plastic wrap) and stand in a warm place for about 1 hour until doubled.

Bake in a hot oven, 220°C/425°F, gas 7 for about 25 minutes. The loaf should sound hollow when tapped on the base and sides. If the top becomes too brown, cover with foil for the last ten minutes.

Bread with macadamias and coconut ▷

SAVOURY ANCHOVY BREAD

Serve this bread, with its pungent flavour of anchovy, garlic and parsley, on its own as a snack, or as an accompaniment to drinks.

Metric/Imperial	Ingredients	American
8 g/2 tsp	Dried (active dry) yeast	2 tsp
1 tsp	Sugar	1 tsp
250 ml/8 fl oz	Warm water	1 cup
400 g/13 oz	Strong white (all-purpose) flour	3 cups
1 tsp	Salt	1 tsp
3 tbsp	Olive oil	3 tbsp
3 tbsp	Finely chopped parsley	3 tbsp
1	Large clove garlic, crushed	1
8	Canned anchovy fillets in oil	8
	Black pepper	

Place the yeast, sugar and warm water in a bowl and stir. Leave to stand for about ten minutes or until some froth has formed on top. Sift the flour and salt into a bowl, make a well in the centre and add the yeast liquid. Mix to a dough. Knead by hand (or in an electric mixer with a dough hook) for seven to ten minutes. Cover with greased or oiled cling film (plastic wrap) and leave in a warm place for about an hour until doubled.

Divide the dough in half. Roll out each piece thinly to form a square about 30 x 30 cm/12 x 12 in. Place one on a greased baking tray (cookie sheet). Brush the top with oil. Mix parsley and garlic and spread or scatter this over the top of the dough as evenly as possible. Drain the anchovies and cut into small pieces. Dot on top and season generously with black pepper.

Place the second piece of dough on top. Pinch lightly at the edges. Using a thick skewer poke holes through at intervals to make a pattern. Brush the top with additional oil. Cover with cling film (plastic wrap) and leave in a warm place for about ten to 15 minutes until the dough has risen a little. Do not let this dough double.

Bake in a hot oven, 220°C/425°F, gas 7 for 15 minutes or until golden on top and crisp. Leave for five minutes before cutting. The bread is best eaten the day it is made.

BREAD WITH TOMATO AND ROSEMARY

Legend has it that rosemary grows only in the gardens of the righteous. This fragrant herb can be easily cultivated as part of a flower garden, or among a bed of other herbs, and is best used fresh when its flavour is more subtle.

Cut into squares, this bread is delicious with soups, salads or meat dishes, or served as an appetizer with drinks.

Metric/Imperial	Ingredients	American
8 g/2 tsp	Dried (active dry) yeast	2 tsp
1 tsp	Sugar	1 tsp
250 ml/8 fl oz	Warm water	1 cup
400 g/13 oz	Strong white (all-purpose) flour	3 cups
1 tsp	Salt	1 tsp
2 tbsp	Olive oil	2 tbsp
1 tbsp	Tomato paste	1 tbsp
1 tbsp	Finely chopped fresh rosemary or	1 tbsp
1 tsp	Dried rosemary	1 tsp
	Black pepper	

Note: If using dried rosemary, put it in warm water for about 15 minutes to soften it slightly. Then cut into pieces if the spikes are large.

Place the yeast and sugar in a bowl, add the water and stir. Leave to stand for about ten minutes or until some froth has formed on top. Sift the flour and salt into a bowl. Make a well in the centre, add the yeast liquid and mix to a dough. Knead by hand (or in an electric mixer with a dough hook) for seven to ten minutes. Cover with greased or oiled cling film (plastic wrap) and leave in a warm place for about an hour until doubled.

Roll the dough out to form a rectangle, about 40 x 15 cm/16 x 6 in or a similar shape to fit in a baking tin or dish with shallow sides. Grease the container.

Whisk the olive oil and tomato paste and brush over the top of the dough, scatter rosemary over the top and season well with black pepper. Make holes with a skewer at intervals. Cover again and leave to rise for about 45 minutes or until doubled.

Bake in a hot oven, 220°C/425°F, gas 7 for about 15 minutes.

Bread with tomato and rosemary ▷

BREAD ENRICHED WITH MILK

Adding milk to white bread gives a fine texture and helps keep the bread fresh. A loaf made with milk as the only liquid would be rather dense, so water is added to lighten the texture.

The dough can be formed into a plain loaf to be used for sandwiches or toast, or it can be shaped into rolls, knots, plaits or whatever takes your fancy.

Metric/Imperial	Ingredients	American
8 g/2 tsp	Dried (active dry) yeast	2 tsp
1 tsp	Sugar	1 tsp
85 ml/3 fl oz	Warm water	⅓ cup
200 ml/6 fl oz	Warm milk	¾ cup
2 tsp	Vegetable oil	2 tsp
500 g/1 lb	Strong white (all-purpose) flour	4 cups
1½ tsp	Salt	1½ tsp

Place the yeast, sugar and warm water in a small bowl and stir. Leave to stand for about ten minutes or until some froth has formed on top. Add the warm milk and vegetable oil. Sift the flour and salt into a bowl. Make a well in the centre, add the yeast liquid and mix to a dough. Knead by hand (or in an electric mixer with a dough hook) for seven to ten minutes. Cover with greased or oiled cling film (plastic wrap) and leave in a warm place for about an hour until doubled in size.

Punch down and form into a loaf. Place in a greased 750 g/1½ lb bread pan. Cover and leave for about 45 minutes until doubled.

Bake in a hot oven, 230°C/450°F, gas 8 for 15 minutes, reduce to 190°C/375°F, gas 5 and bake for a further 15 minutes, covering the top with foil if it becomes too brown.

BREAD STICKS WITH OLIVES

The slightly salty taste of green olives is fresh, yet not too strong in this bread. Stuffed olives, with their contrasting green exterior enclosing little pieces of red pimento are the most attractive variety to use. Stoned black olives could also be used but these have a stronger flavour.

Serve these bread sticks buttered as a snack with drinks, or as an accompaniment to hot meals, cold meats or sliced sausages.

Metric/Imperial	Ingredients	American
8 g/2 tsp	Dried (active dry) yeast	2 tsp
1 tsp	Sugar	1 tsp
285 ml/9 fl oz	Warm water	1 cup + 2 tbsp
500 g/1 lb	Strong white (all-purpose) flour	4 cups
1 tsp	Salt	1 tsp
30	Green olives, stuffed with pimento	30

Place the yeast, sugar and warm water in a small bowl and stir. Leave for about ten minutes or until some froth has formed on top. Sift the flour and salt into a bowl. Make a well in the centre, add the yeast liquid and mix to a dough. Knead by hand (or in an electric mixer with a dough hook) for seven to ten minutes. Cover with greased or oiled cling film (plastic wrap) and leave in a warm place for about an hour until doubled. While the dough is proving chop the olives into very small pieces.

Divide the dough into two equal pieces. Form each piece roughly into an oval. Using a rolling pin, roll out to about 30 x 15 cm/12 x 6 in. Scatter the olives over the top of each piece and press down with your hands so they stick slightly to the top. Roll the dough up as you would a Swiss roll (jelly roll) to enclose the olives. Pinch the join and the ends and turn them slightly under. Place in greased French bread stick pans or on a greased baking tray (cookie sheet) with the join underneath. Cover again and leave in a warm place for about 45 minutes to an hour until doubled.

Bake in a hot oven, 230°C/450°F, gas 8 for about 15 to 20 minutes. Cool on a wire rack.

Bread enriched with milk ▷

CHEESE CRESCENTS

A basket of these herb-flavoured crescents accompanying a bowl of thick soup makes a satisfying winter lunch or supper. On warmer days serve them fresh from the oven with salads, or perhaps with crudités and a bowl of home-made garlicky mayonnaise. Nicest warm, they can be reheated for about five minutes in a moderate oven, 180°C/350°F, gas 4.

Metric/Imperial	Ingredients	American
8 g/2 tsp	Dried (active dry) yeast	2 tsp
1 tsp	Sugar	1 tsp
285 ml/9 fl oz	Warm water	1 cup + 2 tbsp
1 (25 mg)	Ascorbic acid (vitamin C) tablet	1 (25 mg)
500 g/1 lb	Strong white (all-purpose) flour	4 cups
1½ tsp	Salt	1½ tsp
	Filling	
30 g/1 oz	Melted butter or margarine	2 tbsp
125 g/4 oz	Cheddar cheese, grated	1 cup
	Black pepper	
½ tsp	Mixed dried herbs	½ tsp
1	Small egg, beaten with	1
2 tsp	Water	2 tsp

Place the yeast and sugar in a small bowl and add warm water. Crush in ascorbic acid (vitamin C) tablet and stir. Leave to stand for about ten minutes or until some froth has formed on top. Sift the flour and salt into a bowl, make a well in the centre, add the yeast liquid and mix to a dough. Knead by hand (or in an electric mixer with a dough hook) for seven to ten minutes. Cover with greased or oiled cling film (plastic wrap). Leave for 30 to 45 minutes or until doubled in size.

Divide the dough in half and punch down. Roll each into a circle about 30 cm/12 in. Brush with melted butter, scatter with cheese and season with pepper and herbs. Cut each into eight wedges and beginning at the wide end, roll up to form a crescent. Place on two greased baking trays (cookie sheets) with the join underneath. Cover and leave to prove for about 30 minutes or until doubled in size. Brush the top of the crescents with the beaten egg.

Bake in a hot oven, 220°C/425°F, gas 7 for about eight minutes then reduce the oven to 190°C/375°F, gas 5 and bake for a further three to five minutes. The crescents should be light golden brown; do not let them become too dark.

BUTTERY HERB CRESCENTS

Prepare the dough as for Cheese Crescents.

Metric/Imperial	Ingredients	American
	Filling	
30 g/1 oz	Melted butter or margarine	2 tbsp
2 tbsp	Finely chopped parsley	2 tbsp
1 tsp	Finely chopped fresh thyme or	1 tsp
½ tsp	Dried thyme	½ tsp
1 tsp	Finely chopped fresh rosemary or	1 tsp
½ tsp	Dried rosemary, chopped	½ tsp
1 tsp	Finely chopped fresh marjoram or	1 tsp
½ tsp	Dried marjoram	½ tsp
1	Small clove garlic, crushed	1
	Black pepper	

Brush the bread circles with melted butter. Mix the herbs and garlic together and scatter as evenly as possible over the dough. Then grind black pepper on top. Cut into wedges, roll up and bake in the same way as for Cheese Crescents.

HAM CRESCENTS

Prepare the dough as for Cheese Crescents. While the dough is proving for the first time, prepare the filling.

Metric/Imperial	Ingredients	American
	Filling	
45 g/1½ oz	Butter or margarine	3 tbsp
1	Small onion, finely diced	1
250 g/8 oz	Ham, diced	½ lb
1 tbsp	Flour	1 tbsp
¼ tsp	Cayenne pepper	¼ tsp

Melt the butter, add the onion and cook gently until the onion has softened and is transparent. Mince (grind) the ham and add to the pan with onion. Mix in flour and stir well to thicken the mixture. Season with a pinch of cayenne. Leave to cool.

Spread the ham filling over the circles. Cut into wedges, roll up and bake in the same way as for Cheese Crescents.

Cheese crescents ▷

EGG AND BACON PIE

Egg and bacon pie made with pastry is an old favourite; this version has a light, white bread crust and a filling enlivened by the addition of spring onions (scallions). It's a great picnic dish, ideal for a meal or cut into wedges for school lunches. Serve with a tomato and onion or tossed green salad. Though the pie can be reheated, wrapped in foil, it is best served fresh.

Metric/Imperial	Ingredients	American
8 g/2 tsp	Dried (active dry) yeast	2 tsp
1 tsp	Sugar	1 tsp
250 ml/8 fl oz	Warm water	1 cup
400 g/13 oz	Strong white (all-purpose) flour	3 cups
1 tsp	Salt	1 tsp
	Filling	
125 g/4 oz	Bacon slices, diced	4
3 tbsp	Finely chopped parsley	3 tbsp
3 tbsp	Finely chopped spring onions (scallions)	3 tbsp
8	Large eggs	8
	Salt and pepper	

Place the yeast and sugar in a small bowl. Add the warm water and stir. Leave to stand for about ten minutes or until some froth has formed on top. Sift the flour and salt into a bowl. Make a well in the centre, add the yeast liquid and mix to a dough. Knead by hand (or in an electric mixer with a dough hook) for seven to ten minutes. Cover with greased or oiled cling film (plastic wrap) and leave in a warm place for about an hour or until doubled. Punch down the dough and cut about one third away for the top of the pie. Leave the remainder for the base.

Using a rolling pin, roll out the dough into two circles, the larger one to cover the base and sides of a 23 cm/9 in flan case (pie pan), the smaller one to cover the top. Grease the flan case (pie pan) and put the larger piece of dough in the base, pressing it down and into the sides firmly.

Scatter the base with half the bacon, half the parsley and spring onions (scallions). Break the eggs into the crust, season sparingly with salt and generously with pepper. Scatter the remaining bacon, parsley and spring onions (scallions) on top. Using the point of a knife, break the yolk of each egg lightly so that it spreads a little. Carefully place the remaining bread circle on top so as not to disturb the egg. Pinch the edges together and with scissors, cut away any excess bread which would make the crust too thick. Cover and leave in a warm place for about 10 minutes. Do not let this dough prove too much, as the crust should be fairly thin. Glaze the top if you wish with a little beaten egg.

Place in a hot oven, 220°C/425°F, gas 7 and bake for 15 minutes. Reduce to 190°C/375°F, gas 5 and bake a further 20 minutes. Leave to stand for ten minutes before cutting the pie. If using as a cold pie, leave to cool completely and then remove from the pan.

EGG BREAD

This is richer than a plain bread, with a beautiful texture and very fine crumb. Wonderful eaten fresh, it is also excellent toasted when a couple of days old.

Metric/Imperial	Ingredients	American
8 g/2 tsp	Dried (active dry) yeast	2 tsp
½ tsp	Sugar	½ tsp
4 tbsp	Warm water	4 tbsp
500 g/1 lb	Strong white (all-purpose) flour	4 cups
1½ tsp	Salt	1½ tsp
1 tbsp	Skim-milk powder	1 tbsp
30 g/1 oz	Butter or margarine	2 tbsp
3	Eggs	3
	Poppy seeds	

Place the yeast, sugar and warm water in a bowl and stir. Leave to stand until some froth has formed on top. Sift the flour, salt and skim-milk powder into a bowl and rub in the butter until the mixture is crumbly. Beat the eggs, place in a measuring cup and fill up to the 250 ml/8 fl oz (1 cup) level with warm water.

Make a well in the centre of the flour, add the yeast liquid and eggs. Mix to a dough and knead by hand (or in an electric mixer with a dough hook) for seven to ten minutes. Cover with greased or oiled cling film (plastic wrap) and leave in a warm place for about an hour or until doubled.

Punch the dough down and either make a plait or form into two equal-sized balls and place in a 750 g/1½ lb loaf pan. Cover and leave for about an hour or until doubled.

Brush the top with a little water and scatter with poppy seeds. Bake in a hot oven, 230°C/450°F, gas 8 for 15 minutes, reduce the temperature to moderate, 190°C/375°F, gas 5 and bake for a further ten minutes.

Egg and bacon pie ▷

INDIVIDUAL ROUNDS WITH MEAT, PINE NUTS AND TOMATO TOPPING

These little rounds have a tasty topping of lamb or beef with pine nuts and a thin, crisp base. Use lean, finely minced (ground) meat or the finished dish will be too fatty. If carefully packed, the rounds are ideal for school lunches, and are also good eaten cold as a snack on their own or with salads. Keep them on hand in the freezer, but thaw before reheating.

Metric/Imperial	Ingredients	American
8 g/2 tsp	Dried (active dry) yeast	2 tsp
1 tsp	Sugar	1 tsp
285 ml/9 fl oz	Warm water	1 cup + 2 tbsp
500 g/1 lb	Strong white (all-purpose) flour	4 cups
1½ tsp	Salt	1½ tsp
	Topping	
3 tbsp	Olive or vegetable oil	3 tbsp
2	Large onions, finely chopped	2
60 g/2 oz	Pine nuts	½ cup
1	Clove garlic, crushed	1
500 g/1 lb	Finely minced (ground) lamb or lean beef	1 lb
2 tbsp	Finely chopped parsley	2 tbsp
1 tbsp	Lemon juice	1 tbsp
2 tbsp	Tomato paste	2 tbsp
½ tsp	Sugar	½ tsp
¼ tsp	Cinnamon	¼ tsp
	Salt and pepper	

Place the yeast, sugar and warm water in a bowl and stir. Leave to stand until some froth has formed on top. Sift the flour and salt into a bowl. Make a well in the centre, add the yeast liquid and mix to a dough. Knead by hand (or in an electric mixer using a dough hook) for seven to ten minutes. Cover with greased or oiled cling film (plastic wrap) and leave in a warm place for about an hour until doubled.

While the dough is rising prepare the filling. Heat the oil in a frying pan. Add the onions and sauté, stirring occasionally until softened, but not browned. Remove to a bowl. Add the pine nuts to the pan and cook a few minutes or until golden. Watch them as they change colour suddenly. Add garlic and mix, then add to the onion in the bowl. Mix in the lamb or beef, parsley, lemon juice, tomato paste, sugar, cinnamon and season with salt and pepper. The filling should be well mixed.

Divide the dough into about 24 pieces. Form each one into a ball and roll or press out thinly. Place at once on a greased baking tray (cookie sheet). Place a layer of filling over the top of the bread, not quite to the edges and pinch the edge slightly to form a rim.

Place each tray in the oven as it is filled. These rounds should not be left to prove a second time.

Bake in a hot oven, 230°C/425°F, gas 8 for 12 to 15 minutes or until the meat has cooked and the base is crisp. Remove to a rack to cool.

Reheat, wrapped in foil, for five minutes, or wrap them when cooled and freeze. If frozen, thaw before reheating and place in a moderate oven, 190°C/375°F, gas 5 for about seven minutes.

Individual rounds ▷

LEG OF LAMB IN A BREAD CRUST

Meat cooked in a crust is particularly juicy and succulent, but in many recipes this crust is inedible, being made of flour and water with a high proportion of salt added. Here, a leg of lamb, partly roasted to get rid of excess fat, then cooled and covered with a herb butter, is encased in white bread dough. The herb-flavoured bread can be served alongside the meat instead of a potato dish, with vegetables to complete the meal.

The timing given here for the meat leaves it slightly pink. If you prefer it more well done, or are not sure of the tenderness of the lamb, cook for an extra 20 minutes before cooling and wrapping in the bread dough.

Metric/Imperial	Ingredients	American
1 (2 kg/4 lb)	Leg of lamb	1 (4 lb)
30 g/1 oz	Butter or margarine	2 tbsp
	Salt and pepper	
1	Clove garlic, crushed	1
2 tbsp	Finely chopped parsley	2 tbsp
1 tsp	Finely chopped fresh thyme or	1 tsp
¼ tsp	Dried thyme	¼ tsp
1 tbsp	Finely chopped fresh rosemary or	1 tbsp
1 tsp	Dried rosemary	1 tsp
	Dough	
8 g/2 tsp	Dried (active dry) yeast	2 tsp
1 tsp	Sugar	1 tsp
3 tbsp	Warm water	3 tbsp
250 ml/8 fl oz	Additional warm water	1 cup
500 g/1 lb	Strong white (all-purpose) flour	4 cups
1 tsp	Salt	1 tsp
1	Egg, beaten with	1
2 tsp	Water	2 tsp

If the lamb has a thick layer of fat, trim most of this away, especially at the thickest end of the meat. Place in a pan in a moderate oven, 190°C/375°F, gas 5 and cook for about an hour and a half or until the fat is coloured and the meat partly cooked. Remove and leave to cool. Pat the top dry so the butter will stick easily. Remove the shank bone.

Cream the butter with salt, pepper, garlic, parsley, thyme and rosemary. Spread in an even layer over the cooled lamb, or dot here and there if it is easier.

Begin making the dough at least a couple of hours before you wish to eat the lamb. Place the yeast, sugar and three tablespoons of warm water in a bowl and stir. Leave to stand for about ten minutes or until some froth has formed on top, and add the remaining warm water. Sift the flour and salt into a bowl, make a well in the centre, add the yeast liquid and mix to a dough. Knead by hand (or in an electric mixer using a dough hook) for seven to ten minutes. Cover with greased or oiled cling film (plastic wrap) and leave in a warm place for about 45 minutes to an hour, or until doubled.

Punch down the dough and roll out to an oval shape large enough to wrap around the leg. Place the lamb butter side down on the dough and fold the dough over like a parcel to enclose the lamb. Place on a greased flat baking tray (cookie sheet), join downwards. It is best if the tray has a small edge so that if any butter oozes out it will not spill over and smoke in the oven. Cover and leave for about ten minutes to rise slightly, but don't let the dough become too thick. If you wish, glaze before baking with the egg.

Place in a hot oven, 230°C/450°F, gas 8 for 20 minutes. Reduce the oven temperature to 190°C/375°F, gas 5 and bake for a further 25 to 30 minutes, covering the top of the bread with foil if it is becoming too brown. Remove and leave the lamb to stand for five minutes before carving.

To carve, cut through the top of the crust in the centre, break open and remove the meat. Cut the meat into slices and cut a portion of crust for each serving. Do not serve any soggy or wet pieces of dough or the thick parts where it was joined.

Leg of lamb in a bread crust ▷

MEAT PIE

While it may sound unusual, bread dough can be used to make a pie in the same way as pastry. It does not take long to make as the dough is left to rise only once.

    This pie has a crisp, light bread crust holding a moist meat filling. Substantial and delicious, it will serve six to eight people and requires nothing more than a green salad to accompany it.

Metric/Imperial	Ingredients	American
8 g/2 tsp	Dried (active dry) yeast	2 tsp
250 ml/8 fl oz	Warm water	1 cup
400 g/13 oz	Strong white (all-purpose) flour	3 cups
1 tsp	Salt	1 tsp
	Filling	
2 tbsp	Oil	2 tbsp
1	White onion, thinly sliced	1
1	Clove garlic, crushed	1
1	Medium-sized sweet red pepper, seeded and diced	1
500 g/1 lb	Minced (ground) lean beef	1 lb
	Salt and pepper	
2 tbsp	Tomato paste	2 tbsp
1 tbsp	Flour	1 tbsp
125 ml/4 fl oz	Beef or chicken stock	½ cup
1 tsp	Finely chopped fresh thyme or	1 tsp
½ tsp	Dried thyme	½ tsp
3 tbsp	Finely chopped parsley	3 tbsp
1	Large egg, beaten	1
2 tbsp	Currants	2 tbsp
4 tbsp	Grated Parmesan cheese	4 tbsp

Place the dried yeast and warm water in a bowl and stir. Leave to stand for about ten minutes or until some froth has formed on top. Sift the flour and salt into a bowl. Make a well in the centre, add the yeast liquid and mix to a dough. Knead by hand (or in an electric mixer using a dough hook) for seven to ten minutes. Cover with greased or oiled cling film (plastic wrap) and leave for about an hour or until doubled in size.

While the dough is rising prepare the filling. Heat the oil in a large frying pan. Add the onion, garlic and sweet red pepper and cook, stirring occasionally, until the vegetables have softened. Remove to a bowl. Add the beef to the pan and stir until it has changed colour. Season with salt and pepper and add the tomato paste. Mix in the flour and stock, stirring until the mixture has thickened. Mix into the onion and red pepper, add thyme and parsley. Leave to cool slightly, then stir in the egg, currants and cheese.

Lightly grease or oil a deep pie dish (pan), one which holds about 1.75 l/3 pints (7 cups). Divide the dough in half. One piece should be larger than the other. Roll out the larger piece to a circle or oblong and line the base and sides of the pie dish (pan). Fill with the meat. Roll out the remaining section of dough and place on top.

Pinch the edges and trim away excess dough. Crimp or cut small 'v' points with the point of a pair of scissors. Place immediately in a hot oven, 220°C/425°F, gas 7 and bake for 25 minutes, turning it around once if the oven does not cook evenly so the edges will be a uniform golden colour. Remove and place a piece of foil on top. This will soften the crust slightly and make it easier to slice. Leave to stand for 10 minutes before cutting into wedges, or leave to cool completely and serve cold.

Meat pie ▷

31

ONION QUICHE

Meltingly tender, sweet-tasting onions form the basis for this quiche. In France, quiches were originally made with a bread dough, filled with cream and eggs and baked in the village baker's oven. Many fillings have been created for quiches and these days the base is usually made from pastry. However, this recipe for onion quiche is made like the original, with a crisp bread base which is as easy to handle and prepare as any pastry.

Once you have mastered the simple method of preparation, try it with your own favourite fillings.

Metric/Imperial	Ingredients	American
8 g/2 tsp	Dried (active dry) yeast	2 tsp
1 tsp	Sugar	1 tsp
250 ml/8 fl oz	Warm water	1 cup
400 g/13 oz	Strong white (all-purpose) flour	3 cups
1 tsp	Salt	1 tsp
	Filling	
45 g/1½ oz	Butter or margarine	3 tbsp
1 tbsp	Vegetable oil	1 tbsp
750 g/1½ lb	White onion, thinly sliced	1½ lb
2	Large eggs	2
250 ml/8 fl oz	Double (heavy) cream	1 cup
125 g/4 oz	Jarlsburg or Cheddar cheese, grated	1 cup
	Salt and pepper	
90 g/3 oz	Bacon slices	3

Place the yeast and sugar in a bowl, add the warm water and stir. Leave to stand for about ten minutes or until some froth has formed on top. Sift the flour and salt into a bowl, make a well in the centre, add the yeast liquid and mix to a dough. Knead by hand (or in an electric mixer with a dough hook) for about seven to ten minutes. Cover with greased or oiled cling film (plastic wrap) and leave in a warm place for about an hour until doubled.

Lightly grease a baking or roasting pan, about 30 x 23 cm/12 x 9 in. Punch down the dough and roll out to a size slightly larger than the base of the pan. Place in the pan, taking the dough slightly up the sides to form an edge. Cover and leave in a warm place for another 25 minutes. Do not let this double in size or the crust will be too thick.

Melt the butter and oil in a saucepan, sauté the onions, stirring occasionally until slightly softened. Place a lid on the pan, turn the heat to low and leave to cook gently until the onions are quite soft. Leave them to cool slightly before mixing with the eggs.

Beat the eggs to break them slightly, add the cream and mix well. Stir in the onions. Mix in the cheese and season with salt and pepper. The filling can be covered and left at room temperature for several hours. Do not refrigerate because the filling would be too cold when placed on the bread dough. Pour the filling into the bread base and scatter bacon over the top.

Bake in a hot oven, 230°C/425°F, gas 8 for ten minutes. Turn the oven down to 190°C/375°F, gas 5 and bake for a further 15 to 20 minutes or until the centre of the filling is barely set. The quiche is best when slightly creamy in the middle. Do not overcook until firm, because the filling will continue cooking after being removed from the oven. Leave to rest for five minutes before cutting. Using an egg slice, slide the quiche onto a large platter or else cut into eight to ten sections in the baking pan.

To reheat, wrap well in foil and place in a moderately hot oven, 190°C/375°F, gas 5 for about 15 minutes.

Onion quiche ▷

PIZZA ITALIAN

One of the most familiar of all pizzas is the 'Pizza alla Napoletana', a dish which originated in Naples. It always includes tomato in some form, either a fresh tomato sauce or sliced tomato, with cheese, and toppings of anchovies or olives, and perhaps strips of spiced salami. In this version, bacon pieces can be used instead of salami – not strictly Italian, but still very good. Quantities are for two 30 cm/12 in pizzas.

Metric/Imperial	Ingredients	American
8 g/2 tsp	Dried (active dry) yeast	2 tsp
2 tsp	Sugar	2 tsp
285 ml/9 fl oz	Warm water	1 cup + 2 tbsp
500 g/1 lb	Strong white (all-purpose) flour	4 cups
1 tsp	Salt	1 tsp
1 tbsp	Olive oil	1 tbsp
	Tomato Sauce	
1 tbsp	Olive or vegetable oil	1 tbsp
1	Medium-sized onion, finely diced	1
1	Clove garlic, crushed	1
450 g/14 oz	Canned tomatoes in juice	2 cups
1 tbsp	Tomato paste	1 tbsp
1 tsp	Dried oregano	1 tsp
1 tsp	Sugar	1 tsp
	Topping	
250 g/8 oz	Mozzarella cheese, grated	2 cups
125 g/4 oz	Bacon slices, diced	4
	or	
8	Thin salami slices, cut into strips	8
2 tbsp	Olive oil	2 tbsp

First prepare the tomato sauce. Heat the oil in a pan, add the onion and sauté a few minutes until just transparent. Add the garlic. Either put the tomatoes into a food processor for a few seconds to break them up or chop the pieces. Add to the onion with tomato paste, oregano, sugar and cook without a lid for about 25 minutes or until the mixture is a rich, thick sauce. Leave to cool to tepid before using.

Place the yeast and sugar in a bowl, add the water and stir. Leave for about ten minutes or until some froth has formed on top. Sift the flour and salt into a bowl and make a well in the centre. Add the oil to the yeast liquid, pour into the centre of the flour and mix to a dough. Knead by hand (or in an electric mixer with a dough hook) for seven to ten minutes. Cover and leave to rise in a warm place for about an hour until doubled.

Divide the dough in half and roll each piece out to form a circle. Grease two 30 cm/12 in pizza trays with butter; greasing with oil makes the dough slip and it is difficult to keep it in an even circle. Place the dough on the trays and press down, taking it to the edges. Spread with the tomato sauce, dividing evenly between the two rounds. Scatter cheese evenly over this, then the bacon or strips of salami. Lastly trickle a little olive oil on each one.

Place in a hot oven, 220°C/425°F, gas 7 and bake for about 20 to 25 minutes or until the topping has formed a golden melted layer and the base is crisp. Leave to stand for five minutes before cutting.

If you wish you can reheat this in a moderate oven, 180°C/350°F, gas 4 for about eight minutes.

PIZZA BOLOGNESE

Quantities are for two 30 cm/12 in pizza bases, as for Pizza Italian above.

Metric/Imperial	Ingredients	American
	Bolognese Sauce	
2 tbsp	Olive or vegetable oil	2 tbsp
1	Large onion, finely diced	1
1	Bacon slice, finely diced	1
1	Clove garlic, crushed	1
375 g/12 oz	Finely minced (ground) lean beef	¾ lb
1	Bay leaf	1
	Salt and pepper	
425 g/13 oz	Canned tomato soup	1⅔ cups
	Topping	
60 g/2 oz	Mozzarella cheese, grated	½ cup
3 tbsp	Grated Parmesan cheese	3 tbsp
1 tbsp	Oil	1 tbsp

The sauce can be prepared several days beforehand and stored, covered, in the refrigerator. Return to room temperature before using.

Heat the oil in a pan, add the onion and bacon and sauté until the onion has softened. Add garlic and beef and sauté, breaking up the meat with a fork so it does not form lumps. When browned, add the bay leaf, salt and pepper and tomato soup. Cook, uncovered over a gentle heat, stirring occasionally, for about 25 minutes or until it has become a thick sauce.

Make the dough as described above, and place on two pizza trays; brush the top of the dough with a little oil. Spread with the Bolognese topping. Mix the two cheeses together and scatter evenly on top. Lastly, trickle a little extra oil over the top. Bake in a hot oven, 220°C/425°F, gas 7 for 20 to 25 minutes or until the crust is golden and crisp and the topping hot.

Pizza Italian, Pizza Bolognese ▷

POTATO BREAD WITH HERBS

You can add various herbs to this bread. Flavour it with dill to serve with fish or seafood; with rosemary to eat with lamb; or with parsley or thyme to accompany other meats.

Metric/Imperial	Ingredients	American
375 g/12 oz	Potato, finely diced	¾ lb
30 g/1 oz	Butter	2 tbsp
8 g/2 tsp	Dried (active dry) yeast	2 tsp
1 tsp	Sugar	1 tsp
50 ml/2 fl oz	Warm water	Scant ¼ cup
500 g/1 lb	Strong white (all-purpose) flour	4 cups
1 tsp	Salt	1 tsp
2 tbsp	Finely chopped parsley or	2 tbsp
1 tbsp	Finely chopped fresh dill or	1 tbsp
2 tsp	Dried dill	2 tsp

Place the potato in a saucepan, cover with cold water and season with a little salt. Cook, covered until the potato is tender. Drain, and reserve 125 ml/4 fl oz (½ cup) of the water.

Purée the potato, and mix in the reserved potato liquid. While the mixture is still hot, add the butter and mix until it melts. Leave to cool.

Place the yeast and sugar in a small bowl, add the warm water and stir. Leave to stand for about ten minutes or until some froth has formed on top. Sift the flour and salt together and make a well in the centre, add the potato, yeast liquid and parsley or dill to the flour. Mix to a dough. Knead by hand (or use an electric mixer with a dough hook) for seven to ten minutes. If too sticky, add a little more flour. The amount of liquid the dough absorbs will depend on the potatoes. If too dry, add a spoonful or two of tepid water. Cover with greased or oiled cling film (plastic wrap). Leave to stand in a warm place for about an hour or until doubled in size.

Punch down the dough and place in a greased 750 g/ 1½ lb loaf pan. Cover again and leave in a warm place for about an hour until doubled. Bake in a hot oven, 220°C/450°F, gas 8 for 25 minutes or until the bread sounds hollow when tapped on the base and sides.

PUMPKIN BREAD

With its orange-coloured crumb and rich, glazed golden crust, pumpkin bread makes a handsome centrepiece for any table. Serve this moist bread plain with soup, or buttered with hot or cold meats. The unusual pumpkin shape adds interest to the presentation, but form the dough into a more conventional loaf if you prefer.

Metric/Imperial	Ingredients	American
375 g/12 oz	Pumpkin, peeled and chopped	¾ lb
30 g/1 oz	Butter	2 tbsp
1	Small onion, finely diced	1
8 g/2 tsp	Dried (active dry) yeast	2 tsp
1 tsp	Sugar	1 tsp
75 ml/2 fl oz	Warm water	¼ cup
500 g/1 lb	Strong white (all-purpose) flour	4 cups
1½ tsp	Salt	1½ tsp
1	Small egg, beaten with	1
2 tsp	Water	2 tsp

Cook the pumpkin in water until tender. Drain and purée. Melt the butter and sauté the onion until softened.

Place the yeast and sugar in a bowl, add the warm water and stir. Leave to stand for about ten minutes or until some froth has formed on top. Mix the pumpkin and onion together; the mixture should be barely warm. Add to the yeast. Sift the flour and salt into a bowl, make a well in the centre and add the yeast liquid and pumpkin. Mix to a dough. If too sticky, add more flour.

Knead by hand (or in an electric mixer using a dough hook) for seven to ten minutes. Cover with a piece of greased or oiled cling film (plastic wrap) and leave in a warm place for about an hour or until doubled in size.

Punch down the dough. Remove a tiny piece, about the size of a walnut, to form the stem. Form the remainder into a round ball. Flatten this gently and cut about nine slashes around the sides. Roll the small piece of dough to form a stem and place on the centre of the ball. Place on a greased baking tray (cookie sheet), cover again and leave in a warm place for about an hour until doubled.

Glaze with egg and water but not over the cuts. Bake at 220°C/425°F, gas 7 for 25 minutes or until the bread sounds hollow when tapped on the base.

Pumpkin bread ▷

SPINACH, RICOTTA AND CHEESE PIE

Spinach has a natural affinity with cheese, butter, ham or anchovies, and the best seasonings to bring out its flavour are salt, pepper and nutmeg. This pie combines a filling of spinach, creamy fresh ricotta, nutty Jarlsburg and Parmesan cheeses with a white bread crust. It could also be made with wholemeal (whole wheat) flour for a more robust flavour.

It is best to use fresh spinach, which has more texture and a better flavour, but if time is short, use half the quantity of frozen spinach. Cook and drain very well before mixing with the eggs and cheese.

Serve the pie fresh from the oven, warm or cold. It may also be reheated.

Metric/Imperial	Ingredients	American
8 g/2 tsp	Dried (active dry) yeast	2 tsp
1 tsp	Sugar	1 tsp
250 ml/8 fl oz	Warm water	1 cup
400 g/13 oz	Strong white (all-purpose) flour	3 cups
1 tsp	Salt	1 tsp
	Filling	
500 g/1 lb	Fresh spinach	1 lb
3 tbsp	Olive oil	3 tbsp
1	Large onion, finely diced	1
1	Clove garlic, crushed	1
500 g/1 lb	Ricotta cheese	1 lb
1 tsp	Ground black pepper	1 tsp
½ tsp	Salt	½ tsp
90 g/3 oz	Jarlsburg or sharp Cheddar cheese, grated	¾ cup
3 tbsp	Grated Parmesan cheese	3 tbsp
5	Large eggs	5

Place the yeast and sugar in a small bowl. Add the water and stir. Leave to stand for about ten minutes or until some froth has formed on top. Sift the flour and salt into a bowl, make a well in the centre, add the yeast liquid and mix to a dough. Knead by hand (or in an electric mixer using a dough hook) for seven to ten minutes. Cover with a piece of greased or oiled cling film (plastic wrap) and leave in a warm place for about an hour until doubled.

While the dough is standing, prepare the filling. Remove the tough stalks from the spinach. You can leave the spinach leaves whole, even if they are large. Heat the oil in a large frying pan, add the onion and garlic and sauté for a few minutes or until slightly softened.

Wash the spinach well, and add to a large pan with the water that clings to the leaves. If you cannot fit it all in the pan at once, you can do this in batches. Cook until the spinach has softened. Remove and place in a sieve so any liquid will drain away.

Mash the ricotta cheese or place in a food processor and process until smooth. Place in a bowl and add the pepper, salt, Jarlsburg or Cheddar and Parmesan cheese. Add the eggs, retaining a spoonful of egg to glaze the top. Mix well.

Place the spinach on a board and chop it. Add the spinach to the ricotta mixture and stir everything well.

Divide the dough, cutting away one third which will be the top. Roll out the large piece to form a circle sufficiently large to fit into a 1.4 l/3 pint (6 ¼ cups) round or oval pie dish. Grease the dish and press the dough into this, taking it up the sides. Spoon the filling into the dough and smooth the top evenly. Roll out the remaining one third of dough and place over the top. Pinch the edges to join. Trim any excess dough away using scissors.

Brush the top with the reserved spoonful of egg. Place in a hot oven, 230°C/450°F, gas 8 and bake for ten minutes. Reduce to 190°C/350°F, gas 5 and continue baking another 20 to 25 minutes. Remove and leave to stand in the dish for ten minutes before sliding it out. Cut into wedges to serve hot or leave in the dish until cold and wrap in foil to store.

Reheat the pie in a moderate oven, 190°C/350°F, gas 5 for about 20 minutes, or if heating individual slices (wrapped in foil), for about 12 to 15 minutes. Serves eight to ten.

Spinach, ricotta and cheese pie ▷

TANGY CHIVE AND CHEESE BREAD

This moist bread, enriched with cottage cheese and flavoured with chives, is an excellent accompaniment to a variety of soups, salads and meat dishes, and is also good for sandwiches.

Metric/Imperial	Ingredients	American
8 g/2 tsp	Dried (active dry) yeast	2 tsp
½ tsp	Sugar	½ tsp
4 tbsp	Warm water	4 tbsp
500 g/1 lb	Strong white (all-purpose) flour	4 cups
1½ tsp	Salt	1½ tsp
1	Egg, beaten	1
75 ml/3 fl oz	Hot water	⅓ cup
200 g/6 ½ oz	Cottage cheese	1 cup
3 tbsp	Finely chopped chives	3 tbsp

Place the yeast, sugar and warm water in a bowl and stir. Leave to stand for about 10 minutes or until some froth has formed on top. Sift the flour and salt into a basin, make a well in the centre and add the egg. Mix the very hot water into the cottage cheese, stir and add the chives. Pour this into the centre of the flour and mix to a dough. It should be quite moist.

Knead by hand (or in an electric mixer using a dough hook) for seven to ten minutes. Cover with greased or oiled cling film (plastic wrap) and leave to prove in a warm place for about an hour and a half until doubled. This may take a little longer than usual, as the cheese will have lowered the temperature of the dough.

Punch down and divide into halves. Form into two round balls and place in a greased 750 g/1½ lb loaf pan. Cover again and leave in a warm place for about 45 minutes to an hour until doubled.

Glaze the top if you wish with some beaten egg mixed with a little water. Bake in a hot oven, 230°C/450°F, gas 8 for about 15 minutes. Reduce to 190°C/375°F, gas 5 and bake for a further ten to 15 minutes.

TOMATO AND GREEN PEPPERCORN BREAD

The tomato juice gives a pale pink tinge to this loaf, the green peppercorns a spicy flavour. Serve with robust soups, or thinly sliced and buttered to accompany a platter of cold meats.

Metric/Imperial	Ingredients	American
8 g/2 tsp	Dried (active dry) yeast	2 tsp
1 tsp	Sugar	1 tsp
125 ml/4 fl oz	Warm water	½ cup
165 ml/5 fl oz	Tomato juice	⅔ cup
500 g/1 lb	Strong white (all-purpose) flour	4 cups
1 tsp	Salt	1 tsp
2 tsp	Green peppercorns in brine	2 tsp

Place the yeast and sugar in a bowl, add the warm water and stir. Leave to stand for about ten minutes or until some froth has formed on top. Warm the tomato juice to just tepid and add to the yeast. Sift the flour and salt into a bowl, make a well in the centre and add the yeast liquid. Mix to a dough. The thickness of the tomato juice may vary, so add a little more flour when kneading if the dough is too moist. Knead by hand (or in an electric mixer with a dough hook) for seven to ten minutes.

Drain the peppercorns from the brine. Flatten out the dough and spread the peppercorns on top, then knead them in by hand. They will disperse through the bread. Cover with greased or oiled cling film (plastic wrap) and leave in a warm place for about an hour or until doubled.

Punch down and place in a 750 g/1½ lb greased loaf pan. Cover again and leave for about an hour until doubled.

Bake in a hot oven, 220°C/425°F, gas 7 for about 25 minutes or until the bread sounds hollow when tapped on the base and sides.

Tomato and green peppercorn bread ▷

WHOLEMEAL (WHOLE WHEAT) BREAD

WHOLEMEAL (WHOLE WHEAT) BREAD

Wholemeal (whole wheat) bread has grown in popularity over the last few years as people become more concerned about the fibre content of their diets.

This recipe makes a loaf that is full of flavour with a crisp, crunchy crust and a light texture – ideal for those who find some whole-grain breads too heavy. The ingredients are simply flour, yeast, liquid, salt and a little oil and honey. Try to use stone-ground flour if possible, which retains all the goodness of the whole grain. The amount of salt added is a matter of personal taste, but wholemeal (whole wheat) bread without any is rather bland and lacking in flavour.

Glaze the bread just before baking with water or beaten egg and water; top with poppy or sesame seeds, rolled oats or a little extra flour. Slash a pattern in the top of a free-form shape – create plaits, knots or crescents. The choice is yours!

Use the dough, if you like, for a variation on the traditional white pizza base. The finished bread is ideal for healthy sandwiches and excellent toasted.

Metric/Imperial	Ingredients	American
16 g/4 tsp	Dried (active dry) yeast	4 tsp
2 tsp	Honey	2 tsp
630 ml/20 fl oz	Warm water	2½ cups
1 kg/2 lb	Strong wholemeal (whole wheat) flour	8 cups
3 tsp	Salt	3 tsp
1 tbsp	Vegetable oil	1 tbsp

Place the yeast and honey in a small bowl, add the warm water and stir. Leave to stand for about ten minutes or until some froth has formed on top.

Sift the flour and salt into a bowl and return the bran to the flour. Make a well in the centre, add the yeast liquid and oil and mix to a dough. Knead by hand (or in an electric mixer with a dough hook) for seven to ten minutes. Cover with greased or oiled cling film (plastic wrap) and leave in a warm place for about an hour or until doubled in size. Grease a 750 g/1½ lb loaf pan.

Punch down the dough. Form into a loaf or 18 rolls. Cover the loaf or rolls again and leave to prove in a warm place for about 45 minutes to an hour or until doubled in size.

Bake the bread in the centre of a hot oven, 220°C/425°F, gas 7 for about 20 to 35 minutes for a large loaf, 15 minutes for rolls. If any of these should brown too much before they are cooked through, lightly cover with foil. When cooked, the bread should sound hollow when the sides and base are tapped. Leave to cool on a wire rack.

APPLE AND CIDER BREAD

This is not a sweet bread, despite the apple. Spread it with butter or soft cheese, use for pork sandwiches or serve with a platter of fruit and cheese.

Metric/Imperial	Ingredients	American
60 g/2 oz	Dried apple rings, finely chopped	½ cup
315 ml/10 fl oz	Cider	1¼ cups
8 g/2 tsp	Dried (active dry) yeast	2 tsp
1 tsp	Sugar	1 tsp
4 tbsp	Warm water	4 tbsp
500 g/1 lb	Strong wholemeal (whole wheat) flour	3¼ cups
1½ tsp	Salt	1½ tsp

Place the chopped apple in a saucepan with the cider. Bring to a boil and cook gently until the apple has softened slightly. This usually take about five minutes. Leave to cool to tepid. Measure the apple and liquid as some evaporation may occur. It should measure about 300 ml/½ pint (just under 1¼ cups). Make up the amount with warm water if necessary. Put on one side.

Place the yeast and sugar in a bowl, add the warm water and stir. Leave to stand for about ten minutes or until some froth has formed on top. Add the apple and liquid to the yeast.

Sift the flour and salt into a bowl. Return the bran to the flour. Make a well in the centre, add the yeast and apple liquid and mix to a dough. Use your own judgment with this: if too sticky add a few spoonfuls of flour when kneading, if too dry, a spoonful of warm water. Knead by hand (or in an electric mixer using a dough hook) for seven to ten minutes. Cover with greased or oiled cling film (plastic wrap) and leave for about an hour until doubled.

Punch down the dough. Divide into halves and form into two balls. Place in a greased 750 g/1½ lb bread pan and cover again. Leave for about an hour or until doubled.

Bake in a hot oven, 220°C/425°F, gas 7 for about 25 minutes or until the loaf sounds hollow when tapped on the base and sides.

APRICOT BREAD

Fruity, rather than very sweet, this recipe makes a dense loaf which is good with cream cheese. Toasted, it needs only butter, or scatter a few chopped pecan nuts or walnuts on top for a special treat. If you like the combination of sweet and savoury flavours, try it in chicken sandwiches.

Metric/Imperial	Ingredients	American
140 ml/4½ fl oz	Apricot juice (see note)	½ cup
8 g/2 tsp	Dried (active dry) yeast	2 tsp
1 tsp	Honey	1 tsp
170 ml/6 fl oz	Warm water	¾ cup
12	Dried apricots	12
500 g/1 lb	Strong wholemeal (whole wheat) flour	3¼ cups
1 tsp	Salt	1 tsp

Note: Use the juice from a can of apricots in natural syrup. If there is not sufficient juice to make up to 140ml/4½ fl oz (½ cup) use a little extra warm water. For this amount of flour the total liquid should be 310ml/10½ fl oz (1¼ cups).

Place the yeast and honey in a bowl. Add the warm water, stir and leave to stand for about ten minutes or until some froth has formed on top. Place the dried apricots in a bowl, pour boiling water over them and leave to stand two minutes. Drain well and chop apricots into small pieces.

Sift the flour and salt into a bowl and return the bran to the flour. Make a well in the centre. Add the apricot juice to the yeast liquid, tip into the dry ingredients and mix to a dough. Knead by hand (or in an electric mixer using a dough hook) for seven to ten minutes. Add the apricots to the dough and mix to distribute evenly. This is best done by hand. Cover with greased or oiled cling film (plastic wrap) and leave in a warm place for about an hour or until doubled in size.

Punch down the dough. Divide in half. Form the dough into two round loaves, free form, or place in a large greased flower pot or 750 g/1½ lb loaf pan. Cover again and leave in a warm place for about an hour or until doubled.

Bake in a hot oven, 220°C/425°F, gas 7 for 25 to 30 minutes or until the loaf sounds hollow when tapped on the base and sides.

Apricot bread ▷

BREAD WITH SPINACH

Although it is easier to use frozen spinach for this bread, it is worth cooking fresh spinach as the flavour and texture are so much better. Like most vegetable breads this one is very moist and can be served with a variety of foods. Use it in sandwiches with meat, salad or egg fillings; toasted, with scrambled or poached eggs or vegetables in a creamy béchamel sauce, perhaps sprinkled with grated cheese and browned in a hot oven.

Metric/Imperial	Ingredients	American
250 g/8 oz	Fresh spinach	½ lb
1 tbsp	Vegetable or olive oil	1 tbsp
	White pepper	
¼ tsp	Nutmeg	¼ tsp
8 g/2 tsp	Dried (active dry) yeast	2 tsp
1 tsp	Sugar	1 tsp
315 ml/10 fl oz	Warm water	1¼ cups
500 g/1 lb	Strong wholemeal (whole wheat) flour	3¼ cups
1½ tsp	Salt	1½ tsp

Remove the tough or large stalks from the spinach and wash the leaves well. Heat the oil in a frying pan and add the spinach. Cook with the water that clings to the leaves, turning them over several times. Drain very well and chop finely; do not purée. Season with pepper and nutmeg.

Place the yeast and sugar in a bowl. Mix the spinach with the warm water, add to the yeast and stir. Leave to stand for about ten minutes or until some froth has formed on the top. Sift the flour and salt into a bowl and return the bran to the flour. Make a well in the centre and add the yeast and spinach liquid. Mix to a dough. Knead by hand (or in an electric mixer using a dough hook) for seven to ten minutes. Cover with greased or oiled cling film (plastic wrap) and leave in a warm place for about an hour until doubled.

Punch down and form into a loaf. Place into a 750 g/1½ lb greased loaf pan. Cover again and leave in a warm place for about an hour until doubled. Place in a hot oven, 220°C/425°F, gas 7 and cook for 25 minutes or until the loaf sounds hollow when the base and sides are tapped.

BREAD WITH THREE PEPPERS

A combination of green, pink and black peppercorns gives this bread a slightly hot, spicy flavour. Buy them from large supermarkets or delicatessens and rinse the brine away before use. If the pink ones are unobtainable, increase the quantity of green peppercorns to 5 teaspoons.

Use the bread for meat sandwiches, especially beef, or toast it and serve with well-flavoured pâtés, cheese or sautéed mushrooms.

Metric/Imperial	Ingredients	American
8 g/2 tsp	Dried (active dry) yeast	2 tsp
1 tsp	Honey	1 tsp
315 ml/10 fl oz	Warm water	1¼ cups
500 g/1 lb	Strong wholemeal (whole wheat) flour	3¼ cups
1½ tsp	Salt	1½ tsp
2 tsp	Black peppercorns, coarsely crushed	2 tsp
2 tsp	Green peppercorns in brine, drained	2 tsp
1 tbsp	Pink peppercorns in brine, drained	1 tbsp

Place the yeast and honey in a bowl, add warm water and stir. Leave to stand for about ten minutes or until some froth has formed on top. Sift the flour and salt into a bowl. Return the bran to the flour. Make a well in the centre, add the yeast liquid and black peppercorns and mix to a dough. Knead by hand (or in an electric mixer using a dough hook) for seven to ten minutes. Cover with oiled or greased cling film (plastic wrap) and leave in a warm place for about an hour or until doubled.

Flatten out slightly to a round piece. Spread the green peppercorns and pink peppercorns on top of the dough and knead in by hand. Form either into two small loaves or place in a 750 g/1½ lb greased loaf pan. Cover again and leave in a warm place for about an hour until doubled.

Bake in a hot oven, 230°C/450°F, gas 8 for 20 minutes. Reduce to 190°C/375°F, gas 5 and bake for another five minutes if small loaves, another ten minutes if you have made a larger loaf.

Bread with spinach ▷

BUTTERMILK LOAF WITH CHEESE AND BACON

The diced cheese used in this bread melts during baking, so that slices of the finished loaf resemble a Swiss cheese, with small holes formed here and there. The first choice for this is Jarlsburg cheese, which has a good flavour and is not too sticky when melted, but cheeses such as Emmenthal or Gruyère could be used instead.

This bread makes interesting salad sandwiches, is good with sliced tomato on top, delicious with poached or scrambled eggs and makes a nourishing breakfast toasted and served with baked beans.

Metric/Imperial	Ingredients	American
90 g/3 oz	Bacon slices, diced	3
125 g/4 oz	Jarlsburg or similar cheese, diced	1 cup
2 tsp	Finely chopped fresh sage or	2 tsp
¾ tsp	Dried sage	¾ tsp
8 g/2 tsp	Dried (active dry) yeast	2 tsp
1 tsp	Sugar	1 tsp
4 tbsp	Warm water	4 tbsp
500 g/1 lb	Strong wholemeal (whole wheat) flour	3¼ cups
1 tsp	Salt	1 tsp
200 ml/6 fl oz	Buttermilk	¾ cup
75 ml/3 fl oz	Very hot water	⅓ cup

Cook the bacon in a frying pan until it is slightly crisp. Drain it well and mix with the cheese and sage. Place the yeast and sugar in a small bowl, add the warm water and stir. Leave to stand for about ten minutes or until some froth has formed on top.

Sift the flour and salt into a bowl, return the bran to the flour, make a well in the centre and add the yeast liquid. Measure the buttermilk into a jug, add the very hot water and stir. This will take the chill from the buttermilk. Add to the flour and mix to a dough. Knead by hand (or in an electric mixer with a dough hook) for seven to ten minutes.

Flatten the dough slightly, add the cheese and bacon and mix or knead this in by hand. It will be stiff to handle. When the cheese and bacon have been evenly incorporated, cover the dough with greased or oiled cling film (plastic wrap) and leave in a warm place for about an hour until doubled.

Punch down and divide in half. Form two balls and place in a greased 750 g/1½ lb loaf pan. Cover again and leave in a warm place until doubled.

Bake in a hot oven, 220°C/425°F, gas 7 for about 25 minutes. Cover the top with foil if it becomes too brown. Before turning out this loaf, run a knife carefully around the edge as the cheese pieces may stick to the pan.

Buttermilk loaf with cheese and bacon ▷

CURRIED CHICKEN CIRCLE

It is worth buying a chicken and cooking it yourself to make this dish, which has a crusty casing enclosing a light curried filling. If you cannot spare the time, use a ready-cooked chicken and for the sauce use 350 ml/ 12 fl oz (1½ cups) of water and a chicken stock (bouillon) cube instead of the chicken stock.

This makes a very good dinner dish with a cucumber and yoghurt salad and a bowl of mango chutney or some diced banana and fresh cubed pineapple.

Metric/Imperial	Ingredients	American
1 (1.5 kg/3 lb)	Chicken	1 (3 lb)
750 ml/24 fl oz	Water	3 cups
½ tsp	Salt	½ tsp
2	Onion slices	2
A handful	Parsley, including stalks	A handful
3	Hard-boiled (hard-cooked) eggs, coarsely chopped	3
45 g/1½ oz	Butter or margarine	3 tbsp
1	Small onion, finely diced	1
2 tbsp	Flour	2 tbsp
1 level tbsp	Madras (hot) curry powder	1 scant tbsp
350 ml/12 fl oz	Chicken cooking liquid	1½ cups
	Dough	
8 g/2 tsp	Dried (active dry) yeast	2 tsp
1 tsp	Sugar	1 tsp
250 ml/8 fl oz	Warm water	1 cup
400 g/13 oz	Strong wholemeal (whole wheat) flour	2⅔ cups
1 tsp	Salt	1 tsp
1 tbsp	Vegetable oil	1 tbsp

The chicken can be cooked the day before if you wish (cool and refrigerate the chicken and reduced liquid, covered separately, until required). Place the chicken, breast side down, in a saucepan in which it will fit snugly. Add the water: this should come about three-quarters of the way up the chicken. Season with salt, add onion slices and parsley. Bring to a boil, turn the heat to very low, cover and simmer gently for about an hour or until tender. Leave to cool in the liquid. Remove the chicken and strain the liquid. Return the liquid to the heat and boil, uncovered, until reduced to about 350 ml/12 fl oz (1½ cups). Dice the chicken flesh and mix with the eggs.

Melt the butter or margarine in a saucepan, add onion and sauté a few minutes until slightly softened. Add the flour and cook a few minutes, stirring. Add curry powder and fry for 30 seconds or until aromatic. Add the chicken stock and bring to a boil, stirring until thickened. It should be quite a thick mixture. Stir in the diced chicken and chopped egg, and leave to cool. This mixture can be prepared in advance and refrigerated until an hour before use.

For the crust, place the yeast, sugar and warm water in a bowl and stir. Leave to stand for about ten minutes or until some froth has formed on top. Sift the flour and salt into a bowl, and return the bran to the flour. Make a well in the centre and add the yeast liquid and oil. Mix to a dough. Knead by hand (or in an electric mixer using a dough hook) for seven to ten minutes. Cover with greased or oiled cling film (plastic wrap) and leave in a warm place for about an hour or until doubled.

Punch down and form into two equal pieces. Roll each out to a large circle, about 30 cm/12 in in diameter. Place one on a large greased baking tray (cookie sheet) and spread or dot the chicken filling on top. Spread out in a thin, even, layer leaving a strip free around the edge for joining. Place the second circle on top and pinch the edges together well. Trim any excess dough away with scissors

Bake in a hot oven, 220°C/425°F, gas 7 for 15 minutes. Reduce the oven to 190°C/375°F, gas 5 and bake a further ten minutes. Leave to stand for five minutes before cutting in wedges. Serves six generously.

Curried chicken circle ▷

FAMILY-SIZE PASTY (TURNOVER)

Crunchy wholemeal (whole wheat) bread around a meat and vegetable filling makes a more interesting dish than the traditional pasty (turnover). It takes less time to make than a loaf of bread as it needs only one rising. The meat for the filling must be lean, or the finished pasty will be unpleasant when served cold.

This pasty (turnover) is delicious hot with tomato relish and a mixed green salad, and may also be eaten in packed lunches or picnics. Stored in the refrigerator, it keeps well for days.

Metric/Imperial	Ingredients	American
8 g/2 tsp	Dried (active dry) yeast	2 tsp
1 tsp	Honey	1 tsp
315 ml/10 fl oz	Warm water	1¼ cups
500 g/1 lb	Strong wholemeal (whole wheat) flour	3¼ cups
1 tsp	Salt	1 tsp
	Filling	
500 g/1 lb	Finely minced (ground) beef	1 lb
250 g/8 oz	Grated potato	½ lb
250 g/8 oz	Grated carrot	½ lb
1 tsp	Chopped fresh thyme or	1 tsp
½ tsp	Dried thyme	½ tsp
1 tsp	Salt	1 tsp
	Black pepper	
2 tbsp	Finely chopped parsley	2 tbsp
1	Medium-sized onion, finely diced	1
2 tbsp	Tomato chutney or sauce (ketchup)	2 tbsp

Place the yeast and honey in a bowl. Add the warm water and stir. Leave to stand for about ten minutes or until some froth has formed on top. Sift the flour and salt into a bowl. Return the bran to the flour. Make a well in the centre and add the yeast liquid. Mix to a dough. Knead by hand (or in an electric mixer with a dough hook) for seven to ten minutes. Cover with greased or oiled cling film (plastic wrap) and leave in a warm place for about an hour until doubled.

While the dough is rising, prepare the filling. Place the beef in a basin and add potato carrot, thyme, salt, pepper, parsley, onion and chutney. Mix until everything is well blended.

Divide the dough in half and roll out to two ovals. They should be about 30 x 23 cm/12 x 9 in. Place the dough on greased baking trays (cookie sheets) as it is difficult to move once filled.

Divide the meat in half and shape into long thin loaves. Place on the dough, and fold the dough over to enclose the meat. Pinch the dough along the top in a pasty (turnover) shape, pinching and tucking at the ends. Then pleat along the top, making sure the dough is sealed. Trim away any excess dough with scissors. Cover and leave to stand for about five minutes.

Bake in a hot oven, 220°C/425°F, gas 7 for 15 minutes. Reduce to 190°C/375°F, gas 5 and bake for a further 15 to 20 minutes. Leave to stand for five minutes before cutting into thick slices.

To reheat, place in a moderately hot oven, 190°C/375°F, gas 5, for 15 to 20 minutes, depending on the thickness of the pasty (turnover). Individual slices will take about ten minutes. Serves eight to ten.

Family-size pasty (turnover) ▷

FRESH HERB BREAD

Do use fresh herbs for this bread if at all possible; if not, dried ones could be substituted. Aromatic and lightly flavoured with garlic, this bread can be eaten buttered or plain, and is excellent with almost any savoury dish.

Metric/Imperial	Ingredients	American
8 g/2 tsp	Dried (active dry) yeast	2 tsp
1 tsp	Sugar	1 tsp
315 ml/10 fl oz	Warm water	1¼ cups
500 g/1 lb	Strong wholemeal (whole wheat) flour	3¼ cups
1½ tsp	Salt	1½ tsp
4	Cloves garlic, crushed	4
3 tbsp	Finely chopped parsley	3 tbsp
1 tsp	Coarsely ground black pepper	1 tsp
1 tsp	Finely chopped fresh rosemary	1 tsp
1 tbsp	Finely chopped fresh thyme	1 tbsp
1 tsp	Finely chopped fresh marjoram	1 tsp
1 tsp	Finely chopped fresh sage	1 tsp

Note: Halve the quantities of fresh herbs if using dried.

Place the yeast and sugar in a bowl, add the water and stir. Leave to stand for about ten minutes or until some froth has formed on top. Sift the flour and salt into a bowl and return the bran to the flour. Mix the garlic and herbs together and add to the flour. Make a well in the centre, add the yeast liquid and mix to a dough. Knead by hand (or in an electric mixer using a dough hook) for seven to ten minutes. Cover with greased or oiled cling film (plastic wrap). Leave in a warm place for about an hour until doubled in size.

Punch down and divide into two pieces. Roll out and form two long French bread sticks. Place in lightly greased bread stick tins or on a greased baking tray (cookie sheet) and leave for about 45 minutes until doubled.

Bake in a hot oven, 220°C/425°F, gas 7 for about 15 to 20 minutes, depending on the thickness of the sticks.

Reheat in a moderate oven, 180°C/350°F, gas 4 for about seven or eight minutes before serving.

HONEY AND RAISIN BREAD

This bread is excellent cut into thin slices and buttered, to eat with coffee or tea, and is very good toasted for breakfast or supper.

Metric/Imperial	Ingredients	American
8 g/2 tsp	Dried (active dry) yeast	2 tsp
½ tsp	Sugar	½ tsp
4 tbsp	Warm water	4 tbsp
90 g/3 oz	Raisins	½ cup
500 g/1 lb	Strong wholemeal (whole wheat) flour	3¼ cups
1 tsp	Salt	1 tsp
2 tbsp	Honey	2 tbsp
30 g/1 oz	Butter	2 tbsp
	Warm water (see recipe)	
1	Egg	1

Place the yeast, sugar and warm water in a bowl and stir. Leave to stand for about ten minutes until some froth has formed on top. Cut the raisins in half if they are large. Sift the flour and salt into a bowl and make a well in the centre. Place the honey in a saucepan and warm. Add the butter and melt. Place this mixture in a measuring jug and add warm water to bring the level up to 300 ml/10 fl oz (scant 1¼ cups). Pour into the centre of the flour and add the yeast liquid and egg. Mix to a dough. Knead by hand (or use an electric mixer with a dough hook) for seven to ten minutes. Add the raisins and knead or mix in by hand. Cover with greased or oiled cling film (plastic wrap) and leave for about an hour or until doubled.

Punch down the dough, divide in half and form each one into a ball. Place these in a 750 g/1½ lb greased loaf pan, cover and leave about 45 minutes to an hour, or until doubled in size.

Bake in a hot oven, 230°C/450°F, gas 8 for five minutes. Reduce the oven temperature to moderately hot, 190°C/375°F, gas 5 and bake a further 25 minutes or until done.

If you wish, glaze the top of this loaf after it is cooked, with a sugar and water glaze. Mix together equal quantities of sugar and water in a saucepan, heat gently at first to dissolve the sugar, then bring to a boil. Simmer for three minutes until the glaze is syrupy, and brush onto the loaf while still warm.

Fresh herb bread ▷

LETTUCE, SALMON AND SWEET RED PEPPER QUICHE

Salmon is most attractive in this dish, but tuna could be used to make a less expensive meal. A green salad is all that is needed as an accompaniment. Nicest served slightly warm, it can be prepared in advance and reheated if necessary.

Metric/Imperial	Ingredients	American
8 g/2 tsp	Dried (active dry) yeast	2 tsp
1 tsp	Sugar	1 tsp
250 ml/8 fl oz	Warm water	1 cup
400 g/13 oz	Strong wholemeal (whole wheat) flour	2⅔ cups
1 tsp	Salt	1 tsp
	Filling	
60 g/2 oz	Butter or margarine	4 tbsp
1	Large onion, thinly sliced	1
1	Large sweet red pepper, seeded and cut into strips	1
3 packed teacups	Shredded lettuce leaves	3 packed cups
440 g/14 oz	Canned pink or red salmon	14 oz
2	Large eggs	2
170 ml/6 fl oz	Double (heavy) cream	¾ cup
1 tbsp	Tomato paste	1 tbsp
	Salt and pepper	
3 tbsp	Finely chopped spring onions (scallions)	3 tbsp

Place the yeast and sugar in a small bowl, add the warm water and stir. Leave to stand for ten minutes or until some froth has formed on top. Sift the flour and salt into a bowl and return the bran to the flour. Make a well in the centre and add the yeast liquid. Mix to a dough.

Knead by hand (or in an electric mixer using a dough hook) for seven to ten minutes. Cover with greased or oiled cling film (plastic wrap) and leave in a warm place for about an hour until doubled.

Punch down and roll out to an oblong. Grease a large baking tray (cookie sheet) measuring about 43 x 30 cm/ 18 x 12 in. Press the dough into the tin, taking it slightly up the sides. Cover again and leave in a warm place for about 25 minutes until slightly risen. Do not let it double or the crust will be too thick.

Melt half the butter in a pan, add the onion and pepper and sauté, giving an occasional stir, until softened. Remove to a bowl. Add the rest of the butter to the pan. Add the lettuce and stir until softened. Leave to cook gently until tender; this usually takes about ten minutes. Mix with the onion and pepper. Place this mixture on the dough base, and smooth over. Mix the salmon with the eggs, cream and tomato paste and season with salt and pepper. Pour over the lettuce and onion and smooth the top. Scatter the spring onions (scallions) over the surface.

Bake in a hot oven, 220°C/425°F, gas 7 for ten minutes. Reduce to 190°C/375°F, gas 5 and bake for another 20 minutes or until the top has lightly set. Leave to stand for five minutes before cutting.

To reheat, place in a moderate oven, 190°C/375°F, gas 5, uncovered, for 15 to 20 minutes. Serves eight to ten.

VEGETABLE QUICHE

Prepare the base as for Lettuce, Salmon and Sweet Red Pepper Quiche.

Metric/Imperial	Ingredients	American
	Filling	
500 g/1 lb	Courgettes (zucchini)	1 lb
	Salt and pepper	
60 g/2 oz	Butter or margarine	4 tbsp
2 tbsp	Vegetable oil	2 tbsp
1	Large onion, finely diced	1
375 g/12 oz	Grated carrot	¾ lb
½ tsp	Mixed dried herbs	½ tsp
2	Large eggs	2
250 ml/8 fl oz	Double (heavy) cream	1 cup
3	Medium-sized tomatoes	3
45 g/1½ oz	Grated Parmesan cheese	½ cup

The filling may be made several hours before needed, but should not be refrigerated.

Top and tail the courgettes (zucchini) and grate them. Place in a bowl and add two teaspoons salt. Stir and leave to stand for about 20 minutes. Squeeze well.

Melt half the butter and half the oil in a pan. Add the onion and cook until slightly softened. Add the carrot, season and cook until the carrot has softened a little. This should take only about seven minutes. Remove to a bowl, add the rest of the butter and oil to the same pan and cook the courgettes (zucchini), stirring for two minutes. Mix with the carrot and leave to cool. Add the herbs, eggs and cream and stir.

Spread the filling over the dough base and smooth the top. Slice the tomatoes and arrange on top, season with salt and pepper and scatter cheese over the surface. Bake in a hot oven, 230°C/450°F, gas 8 for ten minutes, reduce to 190°C/375°F, gas 5 and bake until the topping has set. This usually takes another 15 minutes. Do not let the filling become too firm; it should be lightly set, as it continues cooking after being taken from the oven. Rest the quiche for five minutes before cutting. It can be removed easily from the baking tin or cut into squares in the tin

To reheat, wrap in foil and place in a moderate oven, 180°C/350°F, gas 4 for about 15 minutes. Serves eight to ten.

Lettuce, salmon and sweet red pepper quiche ▷

TOMATO AND CHEESE SLICE

This attractive tart combines tomatoes with two different cheeses and a substantial bread base. Very good eaten straight from the oven, it can also be served cold on the day it is made. As a meal with perhaps a green salad it makes eight generous servings, or it can be used, cut into tiny pieces, as a piquant appetizer.

Metric/Imperial	Ingredients	American
8 g/2 tsp	Dried (active dry) yeast	2 tsp
1 tsp	Honey	1 tsp
250 ml/8 fl oz	Warm water	1 cup
400 g/13 oz	Strong wholemeal (whole wheat) flour	2⅔ cups
1 tsp	Salt	1 tsp
	Topping	
1 tbsp	Olive oil	1 tbsp
200 g/7 oz	Jarlsburg or Mozzarella cheese	1¾ cups
750 g/1½ lb	Tomatoes	1½ lb
	Salt and pepper	
1 tsp	Sugar	1 tsp
2 tbsp	Chopped fresh basil or	2 tbsp
2 tsp	Dried basil or oregano	2 tsp
3 tbsp	Finely chopped spring onions (scallions)	3 tbsp
90 g/3 oz	Grated Parmesan cheese	¾ cup

Place the yeast and honey in a bowl. Add the warm water and stir. Leave to stand for about ten minutes or until some froth has formed on top. Sift the flour and salt into a bowl and return the bran to the flour. Make a well in the centre, add the yeast liquid and mix to a dough. Knead by hand (or in an electric mixer using a dough hook) for seven to ten minutes. Cover with greased or oiled cling film (plastic wrap) and leave in a warm place for about an hour or until it has doubled in size.

Grease a large baking tray (cookie sheet) or roasting pan measuring about 43 x 30 cm/15 x 12 in. Punch down the dough and roll out to fit the tin, taking it slightly up the edges to form a rim. Cover again and leave in a warm place for about 25 minutes or until slightly risen. Do not let this double or it will be too thick.

Brush the bread dough with oil. Cut the cheese into thin slices: this is better than grating as it makes a layer which prevents the crust becoming soggy. Place the cheese over the dough to cover it completely.

Cut the tomatoes into slices and arrange over the cheese, overlapping them slightly. Season with salt, pepper and sugar. Scatter the top with either basil or oregano, spring onions (scallions), then lastly with an even layer of grated Parmesan cheese.

Bake in a hot oven, 230°C/450°F, gas 8 for 15 minutes. Reduce to 190°C/375°F, gas 5 and bake a further ten minutes. The cheese topping should be melted. Leave to stand for five minutes before cutting. Any moisture which has come from the tomatoes will settle in this time.

Although this dish is best eaten when freshly made, it can be reheated uncovered in a moderately hot oven, 190°C/375°F, gas 5 for a short time until warmed through.

Note: In summer when tomatoes are very juicy, drain the slices on kitchen paper before placing them on the base, to remove some of the moisture which could make the mixture too wet.

Tomato and cheese slice ▷

VEGETARIAN PIZZA

A tasty, Mediterranean-style topping of onions, sweet peppers, mushrooms and tomatoes, on a wholemeal (whole wheat) bread base, scattered with grated cheese and baked to golden perfection, makes this a dish that meat-eaters as well as vegetarians will love.

Metric/Imperial	Ingredients	American
8 g/2 tsp	Dried (active dry) yeast	2 tsp
1 tsp	Honey	1 tsp
315 ml/10 fl oz	Warm water	1¼ cups
500 g/1 lb	Strong wholemeal (whole wheat) flour	3¼ cups
1 tsp	Salt	1 tsp
	Topping	
4 tbsp	Olive or vegetable oil	4 tbsp
2 tbsp	Tomato paste	2 tbsp
45 g/1½ oz	Butter or margarine	3 tbsp
2	Large onions, thinly sliced	2
1	Large sweet red or green pepper, seeded and cut into strips	1
1	Large clove garlic, crushed	1
375 g/12 oz	Mushrooms, thinly sliced	¾ lb
	Salt and pepper	
500 g/1 lb	Tomatoes	1 lb
3 tbsp	Grated Parmesan cheese	3 tbsp
60 g/2 oz	Grated Mozzarella cheese	½ cup

Place the yeast and honey in a bowl. Add the warm water and stir. Leave to stand for about ten minutes or until some froth has formed on top. Sift the flour and salt into a bowl and return the bran to the flour. Make a well in the centre, add the yeast liquid and mix to a dough. Knead by hand (or in an electric mixer using a dough hook) for seven to ten minutes. Cover with greased or oiled cling film (plastic wrap) and leave in a warm place for about an hour until doubled.

Prepare the topping while the dough is rising. Mix half the oil with the tomato paste and leave on one side. Melt the butter in a large frying pan, add the onion and sweet pepper and sauté, stirring occasionally, until softened. Add the garlic and fry for one minute. Put the contents of the pan in a bowl. Use the same pan to cook the mushrooms, but do not add more butter. Season well and fry for two minutes until softened. Mix with the onion.

Divide the dough in half. Roll out each piece to form a circle and place in a lightly buttered 30 cm/12 in pizza tray, taking it right to the edges and pressing down firmly. Spread the oil and tomato paste over the dough with a pastry brush. Divide the vegetable filling into two and spread it over the pizzas, taking it right to the edges. Thinly slice the tomatoes and place in a circle round the edge of the pizzas. Season with salt, pepper and, if the tomatoes have little flavour, half a teaspoon of sugar. Mix the two cheeses and scatter evenly on top. Trickle the rest of the oil over the cheese.

Bake in a hot oven, 220°C/450°F, gas 7 for about 20 to 25 minutes or until the top is golden and the crust crisp.

WALNUT BREAD

This recipe is based on the walnut breads of France, where it is a custom to eat the young, new season's nuts with a glass of wine, some coarse salt and good bread. The walnut oil used in this bread adds a unique flavour, but is very expensive, so use a light vegetable oil instead if you feel it is too extravagant. Choose light-coloured (English) walnuts rather than the black (American) variety which taste too bitter when baked; or substitute pecans.

Serve the bread with cheese, as a base for chicken sandwiches or with sliced ripe banana.

Metric/Imperial	Ingredients	American
8 g/2 tsp	Dried (active dry) yeast	2 tsp
1 tbsp	Honey	1 tbsp
300 ml/10 fl oz	Warm water	1¼ cups
2 tbsp	Walnut oil	2 tbsp
500 g/1 lb	Strong wholemeal (whole wheat) flour	3¼ cups
1½ tsp	Salt	1½ tsp
60 g/2 oz	Walnuts, coarsely chopped	½ cup
	Topping	
1	Egg, beaten with	1
2 tsp	Water	2 tsp
1 tbsp	Walnuts, finely chopped	1 tbsp

Place the yeast, honey and warm water in a bowl. Stir. Leave to stand for ten minutes or until some froth has formed on top. Add the walnut oil. Sift the flour and salt into a bowl and return the bran to the flour. Make a well in the centre and add the yeast liquid and walnuts. Knead by hand (or in an electric mixer using a dough hook) for seven to ten minutes. Cover with greased or oiled cling film (plastic wrap) and leave to stand in a warm place for about an hour or until doubled.

Punch down the dough. Form into a loaf and place in a 750 g/1½ lb loaf pan or two oiled and well-seasoned flower pots. Cover again and leave in a warm place for about an hour or until doubled.

Brush the top of the loaf with egg. Scatter the walnuts on top. Bake in a hot oven, 220°C/425°F, gas 7 for about 20 minutes if in individual flower pots, 30 minutes if in a loaf pan.

Walnut bread ▷

62

SEED AND GRAIN BREAD

SEED AND GRAIN BREAD

This bread is moist, with a chewy texture and good crust. It is dark in colour and flecked with seeds and grain.

In the recipe, some of the grains are heated first with water to soften them, others are added to the flour. You will find the dough quite firm to handle and knead, because of the density of the mixture, and somewhat sticky. Do not add any extra flour when kneading until all the ingredients are well mixed. Sometimes, as the dough is kneaded, some of the moisture is absorbed by the grains, but if it is still too sticky after a few minutes, knead in a little extra wholemeal (whole wheat) flour to get the right consistency. To make a lighter bread use 250 g/8 oz (2 cups) of white flour to 750 g/1½ lb (4⅔ cups) of wholemeal (whole wheat) flour. The bread will still be very nutty and brown, but the dough will be easier to handle.

Because of its density this bread takes longer to prove and will not reach the same volume as white or wholemeal (whole wheat) bread. Be patient and leave it to rise in a gentle warmth, relying on your own judgment rather than strict timing.

Like other breads, this one is not so tasty without some salt, but the lack of salt will be less obvious because of the nuttiness of the mixture. Glaze the top with water, or with beaten egg mixed with water before baking, and top with more seeds, rolled oats or bran. Make sure the bread is cooked before you take it out of the oven; it may feel firm, yet still be too moist in the centre. If the base and sides sound hollow when tapped, the loaf is done.

If you are concerned with healthy living, seed and grain bread could form a useful part of a low-sodium diet, or one where you are trying to increase your fibre intake.

Metric/Imperial	Ingredients	American
2 tbsp	Cracked wheat	2 tbsp
2 tbsp	Millet seeds	2 tbsp
350 ml/11 fl oz	Warm water	1⅓ cups
2 tsp	Molasses	2 tsp
1 tbsp	Vegetable oil	1 tbsp
12 g/3 tsp	Dried (active dry) yeast	3 tsp
2 tbsp	Wheat germ	2 tbsp
1 tbsp	Sunflower seeds	1 tbsp
2 tbsp	Flax seeds	2 tbsp
1 tbsp	Sesame seeds	1 tbsp
500 g/1 lb	Strong wholemeal (whole wheat) flour	3¼ cups
1½ tsp or less	Salt	1½ tsp or less

Place the cracked wheat and millet seeds in a saucepan with the water. Bring to a boil and immediately remove from the heat. Add the molasses and stir to dissolve. Leave to cool until tepid. Add the vegetable oil. Place the yeast in a bowl, add the liquid and stir. Leave to stand until some froth has formed on top.

Place wheat germ, sunflower seeds, flax and sesame seeds in a large basin. Sift the wholemeal (whole wheat) flour and salt on top of the seeds and return the bran to the flour. Mix well. Make a well in the centre, add the yeast liquid and mix to a dough. It will be firm, but should also be very moist. If dry, add a few spoonfuls of warm water; if too wet, add a little more wholemeal (whole wheat) flour as you knead.

Knead by hand (or in an electric mixer using a dough hook) for seven to ten minutes. Leave to prove in a warm place, covered with greased or oiled cling film (plastic wrap). It takes longer than white or a plain wholemeal (whole wheat) dough, so allow about an hour and a half to two hours. Punch down the dough, divide in half and shape into two balls. Place in a greased 750 g/1½ lb loaf pan. Cover again and leave for about an hour to an hour and a half until doubled.

Glaze the top if desired with some beaten egg mixed with water or with lukewarm water, and top with seeds, oatmeal or bran. Place in a hot oven, 230°C/450°F, gas 8 for ten minutes. Reduce to 190°C/375°F, gas 5 and bake for a further 20 to 25 minutes, or until the loaf sounds hollow when the base and sides are tapped.

BANANA BREAD

Allow plenty of time for this bread to prove, as the addition of bananas makes it rise more slowly than plainer breads. Serve with curried or spiced vegetable dishes.

Metric/Imperial	Ingredients	American
8 g/2 tsp	Dried (active dry) yeast	2 tsp
2 tsp	Honey	2 tsp
4 tbsp	Warm water	4 tbsp
375 g/12 oz	Strong wholemeal (whole wheat) flour	2⅓ cups
125 g/4 oz	Strong white (all-purpose) flour	1 cup
1 tsp	Salt	1 tsp
1 tbsp	Skim-milk powder	1 tbsp
1 tbsp	Sunflower seeds	1 tbsp
1 tbsp	Sesame seeds	1 tbsp
1 tbsp	Cracked wheat	1 tbsp
2	Medium-sized ripe bananas, peeled and mashed	2
	Warm water (see recipe)	

Place the yeast, honey and warm water in a small bowl and stir. Leave to stand for about five minutes or until some froth has formed on top. Sift the flours, salt and skim-milk powder into a bowl and return the bran to the flour. Add the sunflower seeds, sesame seeds and cracked wheat.

Pour the yeast mixture into a measuring jug, add the mashed banana and top up with warm water to make it up to 300 ml/10 fl oz (scant 1¼ cups). Make a well in the centre of the flour, add the yeast and banana liquid and mix to a dough. The moisture in the banana can vary, so if the dough is too sticky, add a little more flour while kneading; if dry, moisten with more warm water. Knead by hand (or in an electric mixer using a dough hook) for seven to ten minutes. Cover with greased or oiled cling film (plastic wrap) and leave in a warm place for about an hour and a half until doubled.

Punch down the dough, divide and form into two balls. Place these in a 750 g/1½ lb greased loaf pan and cover again. Leave to prove for about an hour until doubled.

Bake in a hot oven, 220°C/425°F, gas 7 for about 25 to 30 minutes. If the top browns too quickly, cover loosely with foil.

BREAD WITH MUSTARD AND SPRING ONIONS (SCALLIONS)

This lightly spiced bread is moist and looks most attractive. It is delicious with meat, cheese or soup, or buttered for a snack.

Metric/Imperial	Ingredients	American
8 g/2 tsp	Dried (active dry) yeast	2 tsp
1 tsp	Sugar	1 tsp
5 tbsp	Warm water	5 tbsp
2 tbsp	Millet seeds	2 tbsp
2 tbsp	Cracked wheat	2 tbsp
250 ml/8 fl oz	Water	1 cup
2 tsp	English mustard powder	2 tsp
1 tbsp	Prepared French or Dijon mustard	1 tbsp
375 g/12 oz	Strong wholemeal (whole wheat) flour	2⅓ cups
125 g/4 oz	Strong white (all-purpose) flour	1 cup
1½ tsp	Salt	1½ tsp
1 tbsp	Sunflower seeds	1 tbsp
2 tbsp	Flax seeds	2 tbsp
3 tbsp	Finely chopped spring onions (scallions)	3 tbsp

Place the yeast, sugar and warm water in a small bowl and stir. Leave to stand for about ten minutes or until some froth has formed on top. Place the millet seeds and cracked wheat in a saucepan with the 250 ml/8 fl oz (1 cup) water and bring to a boil. Turn off the heat and leave to cool until tepid. Add both the mustards to the liquid. Mix into the yeast.

Sift the flours and salt into a bowl and return the bran to the flour. Mix in sunflower and flax seeds and spring onions (scallions). Make a well in the centre, add the yeast liquid and mix to a dough. You may have to knead in a little extra flour or, if the liquid reduced when the millet was boiled, add a little extra liquid. Knead by hand (or in an electric mixer using a dough hook) for seven to ten minutes. Cover with greased or oiled cling film (plastic wrap) and leave for about an hour and a half until doubled.

Punch down the dough and divide into 12 pieces. Form each into a ball, then flatten and roll up to form an oblong piece. Place these one at a time in a 750 g/1½ lb greased loaf pan, pressing them together firmly. Cover and leave to stand for about an hour in a warm place until doubled.

Bake in a hot oven, 230°C/450°F, gas 8 for 15 minutes. Reduce to moderately hot, 190°C/375°F, gas 5 and bake a further ten to 15 minutes.

Bread with mustard and spring onions (scallions) ▷

MUSHROOM AND WHITE WINE CIRCLE

Two thin, crisp layers of bread enclose a rich, creamy mushroom filling in a pie that is special enough to serve as a first course at a dinner party. Prepare in advance and reheat when required if this is more convenient.

Metric/Imperial	Ingredients	American
8 g/2 tsp	Dried (active dry) yeast	2 tsp
1 tsp	Honey	1 tsp
250 ml/8 fl oz	Warm water	1 cup
250 g/8 oz	Strong wholemeal (whole wheat) flour	1½ cups
125 g/4 oz	Strong white (all-purpose) flour	½ cup
1 tsp	Salt	1 tsp
1 tbsp	Cracked wheat	1 tbsp
1 tbsp	Flax seeds	1 tbsp
1 tsp	Sesame seeds	1 tsp
	Filling	
45 g/1½ oz	Butter or margarine	3 tbsp
1	Large onion, finely diced	1
500 g/1 lb	Mushrooms, thinly sliced	1 lb
125 ml/4 fl oz	Dry white wine	½ cup
	Salt and pepper	
1 tbsp	Flour	1 tbsp
125 ml/4 fl oz	Double (heavy) cream	½ cup
1	Egg	1
	Glaze	
1	Egg, beaten with	1
2 tsp	Water	2 tsp

Place the yeast, honey and warm water in a bowl and stir. Leave to stand for about ten minutes or until some froth has formed on top. Sift the two flours and salt into a bowl and return the bran to the flour. Add the cracked wheat, flax and sesame seeds. Make a well in the centre, add the yeast liquid and mix to a dough. Knead by hand (or in an electric mixer using a dough hook) for seven to ten minutes. Cover with greased or oiled cling film (plastic wrap) and leave for about an hour and a half in a warm place or until doubled.

Prepare the filling so it will have time to cool while the dough is proving. Melt the butter, add onion and cook gently until softened and pale golden. Remove to a bowl. Add the mushrooms to the pan (there should be sufficient moisture to cook them), and fry for a few minutes until softened. Add the wine and cook rapidly until the liquid has evaporated. Season with salt and pepper. Combine the flour, cream and egg. Add this to the mushrooms, stirring. The mixture should thicken in a few minutes. Mix in the cooked onion and place in a bowl to cool.

Divide the proved dough in half. Form each into a round and roll out to form a 30 cm/12 in circle. Place one of the circles on a large greased baking tray (cookie sheet). Dot the cooled mushroom filling over this, spreading it out close to the edges. Leave a small edge free for sealing the crusts together.

Place the second circle of dough over the top. Join the edges, pinching them together. Trim away any excess with scissors. If you wish, glaze the top with beaten egg. Cover and leave to stand for five minutes, but don't let this prove for long or it will be too thick.

Bake in a hot oven, 220°C/425°F, gas 7 and cook for 15 minutes. Reduce to 190°C/375°F, gas 5 and bake for a further ten to 15 minutes. It should be quite crisp on top. Leave to rest for five minutes before cutting into slices.

To reheat, cover with foil and place in a moderately hot oven, 190°C/375°F, gas 5 for 15 minutes.

Serves six as a main course, ten as a first course.

Mushroom and white wine circle ▷

ROLLED ONION BREAD

For this bread, a layer of onion and cheese is spread over the base, which is then rolled up like a Swiss roll (jelly roll). Use to accompany grilled meats, soups or cheese.

Metric/Imperial	Ingredients	American
8 g/2 tsp	Dried (active dry) yeast	2 tsp
2 tsp	Honey	2 tsp
280 ml/9 fl oz	Warm water	1 cup + 2 tbsp
275 g/12 oz	Strong wholemeal (whole wheat) flour	2⅓ cups
125 g/4 oz	Strong white (all-purpose) flour	1 cup
1½ tsp	Salt	1½ tsp
1 tbsp	Wheat germ	1 tbsp
1 tbsp	Sunflower seeds	1 tbsp
2 tsp	Skim-milk powder	2 tsp
1 tbsp	Flax seeds	1 tbsp
1 tbsp	Vegetable oil	1 tbsp
	Filling	
30 g/1 oz	Butter	2 tbsp
1	Medium-sized onion, finely diced	1
1	Clove garlic, crushed	1
4 tbsp	Grated Parmesan cheese	4 tbsp

Place the yeast, honey and warm water in a bowl and stir. Leave to stand until some froth has formed on top. Sift the flours with salt into a bowl and return the bran to the flour. Add the wheat germ, sunflower seeds, skim-milk powder and flax seeds. Make a well in the centre, add the yeast liquid and oil and mix to a dough. Knead by hand (or in an electric mixer using a dough hook) for seven to ten minutes. Cover with greased or oiled cling film (plastic wrap) and leave in a warm place for an hour and a half until doubled.

Prepare the filling while the dough is proving so that it has time to cool. Melt the butter in a small pan, add the onion and sauté, stirring occasionally until it has softened and turned pale gold. Add the garlic and cook for 30 seconds. Remove from the heat, cool a little and mix in the Parmesan cheese.

Punch down the dough and form into a rough oval about 30 x 20 cm/12 x 8 in. Spread the onion filling over the top and roll over lengthways, turning over firmly so the filling is enclosed. Seal the seam with your fingers. Place on a greased baking tray (cookie sheet) join side downwards, and press the ends together or tuck neatly underneath. Cover and leave for about an hour in a warm place until almost doubled.

Bake in a hot oven, 230°C/450°F, gas 8 for 15 minutes, reduce to 190°C/375°F, gas 5 and continue baking for another 15 minutes. Cover the top with foil if it is browning too much. Cool on a rack.

YOGHURT AND GINGER BREAD

Apart from adding flavour to food, ginger has many other uses and was once reputed to 'warm and improve the circulation'. Here it is used in an aromatic bread that is best made with grated fresh green ginger, but is still very good if made with the powdered spice. It takes a little longer to prove than some other breads because of the yoghurt, which enriches the dough and gives the finished loaf a moist texture.

Metric/Imperial	Ingredients	American
8 g/2 tsp	Dried (active dry) yeast	2 tsp
1 tsp	Honey	1 tsp
75 ml/3 fl oz	Warm water	⅓ cup
375 g/12 oz	Strong wholemeal (whole wheat) flour	2⅓ cups
125 g/4 oz	Strong white (all-purpose) flour	1 cup
1½ tsp	Salt	1½ tsp
1 tbsp	Cracked wheat	1 tbsp
1 tbsp	Flax seeds	1 tbsp
1 tsp	Ground coriander	1 tsp
2 tsp	Grated fresh (green) ginger or ground ginger	2 tsp
4 tbsp	Hot water	4 tbsp
50 ml/5 fl oz	Natural (unflavored) low-fat yoghurt	⅔ cup

Mix the yeast with the honey and warm water and stir. Leave to stand for about ten minutes or until some froth has formed on top. Sift the two flours with salt into a bowl and return the bran to the flour. Add cracked wheat, flax seeds, coriander and ginger to the flour. Make a well in the centre and add the yeast liquid. Mix the very hot water with the yoghurt and add to the flour. Mix to a dough.

Knead by hand (or in an electric mixer using a dough hook) for seven to ten minutes. Cover with greased or oiled cling film (plastic wrap) and leave in a warm place for about two hours until doubled.

Punch down the dough and either form into a round, free-form loaf or place in a 750 g/1½ lb greased loaf pan. Cover again and leave for about an hour until doubled.

Place in the centre of a hot oven, 230°C/450°F, gas 8 and bake for 15 minutes. Reduce to 190°C/375°F, gas 5 and bake for a further 15 minutes or until the loaf sounds hollow when tapped on the base and sides.

Rolled onion bread ▷

LIGHT RYE BREAD

LIGHT RYE BREAD

Rye breads have a close, dense texture and make an interesting change from other breads. The flavour is slightly sharp, almost sour, making the bread an ideal partner for cheese or smoked fish.

Do not expect rye bread to reach great heights when proving and baking. The dough is firm and *will* rise, but not to the same degree as a white or wholemeal (whole wheat) loaf. Both dark and light rye flours are available and should always be used combined with white flour because of their low gluten content. All these recipes use light rye flour.

If the dough is too hard to knead, add some warm water; if too moist, a little extra white flour. It should be firm and elastic but not wet. Knead thoroughly, especially if you are doing this by hand and be patient when proving the dough. The finished bread will be far more successful if allowed to rise unhurried in a gentle warmth.

Traditionally this bread is made in a long, oval shape with the top slashed across in several places. Bake it plain, or glaze the top with water or egg beaten with water and sprinkle with caraway seeds just before it goes into the oven. Rye bread keeps well and is best served thinly sliced.

Metric/Imperial	Ingredients	American
16 g/4 tsp	Dried (active dry) yeast	4 tsp
2 tsp	Honey	2 tsp
575 ml/19 fl oz	Warm water	2⅓ cups
500 g/1 lb	Strong white (all-purpose) flour	4 cups
500 g/1 lb	Rye flour	3½ cups
3 tsp	Salt	3 tsp

Place the yeast, honey and water in a bowl and stir. Leave to stand for ten minutes or until some froth has formed on top. Sift the flours and salt into a bowl, and return any bran to the bowl. Make a well in the centre of the flour, add the yeast liquid and mix to a dough. Knead by hand (or in an electric mixer using a dough hook) for seven to ten minutes. Cover with greased or oiled cling film (plastic wrap) and leave in a warm place for about an hour to an hour and a half or until doubled.

Punch down the dough. This quantity will make two large loaves, or three oval free-form shapes. Place the loaves on a greased baking tray (cookie sheet) or into greased 500 g/1 lb loaf pans. Cover again and leave for at least an hour until almost doubled.

Bake in a hot oven, 230°C/450°F, gas 8 for 15 minutes, reduce to 190°C/375°F, gas 5 and bake for a further 15 minutes if you have made two large loaves, ten minutes if baking three oblong loaves. Cool on a wire rack.

BEER BREAD

Beer gives a light texture and tang to this bread.
Honey is added, not to sweeten the bread but to
counteract the slight bitterness which beer imparts.
Use a light beer, not one which is too malty and heavy.
The bread is very good with fish, particularly smoked
fish, and is also excellent with oysters.

Metric/Imperial	Ingredients	American
8 g/2 tsp	Dried (active dry) yeast	2 tsp
1 tbsp	Honey	1 tbsp
4 tbsp	Warm water	4 tbsp
250 g/8 oz	Strong white (all-purpose) flour	2 cups
250 g/8 oz	Rye flour	1¾ cups
1½ tsp	Salt	1½ tsp
150 ml/5 fl oz	Light beer	⅔ cup
75 ml/3 fl oz	Boiling water	⅓ cup

Place the yeast, honey and warm water in a small bowl
and stir. Leave to stand for about ten minutes or until
some froth has formed on top. Sift the flours with salt
into a bowl and return the bran to the flour. Make a well
in the centre of the flour and add the yeast liquid.

Measure the beer and if it has a head on top wait until
this subsides to check the measurement. Add the boiling
water to the beer to warm it slightly and tip into the flour.
Mix to a dough. Knead by hand (or in an electric mixer
using a dough hook) for seven to ten minutes. Cover with
greased or oiled cling film (plastic wrap) and leave in a
warm place for about an hour or until doubled.

Punch down the dough and divide in half. Shape each
piece into a round ball and place in a greased 750 g/1½ lb
loaf pan. This will not be a high loaf, so if you wish for a
taller one, place in a 500 g/1 lb pan. Leave until doubled.

Bake in a hot oven, 230°C/450°F, gas 8 for 15 minutes.
Reduce to 190°C/375°F, gas 5 for a further 15 minutes.

BLACK BREAD

The recipe for this dense black bread has been adapted
from one popular in the United States. Cocoa and
coffee powder are used to darken rather than flavour it.
Serve with strong cheeses, smoked meats and dill
pickles.

Metric/Imperial	Ingredients	American
8 g/2 tsp	Dried (active dry) yeast	2 tsp
285 ml/9 fl oz	Warm water	1 cup + 2 tbsp
250 g/8 oz	Rye flour	1¾ cups
250 g/8 oz	Strong white (all-purpose) flour	2 cups
1 tbsp	Cocoa powder	1 tbsp
1 tbsp	Instant coffee powder	1 tbsp
1 tbsp	Dark brown sugar	1 tbsp
1 tsp	Salt	1 tsp
30 g/1 oz	Melted butter	2 tbsp
	Glaze	
1	Egg white	1
1 tbsp	Water	1 tbsp

Place the yeast in a bowl, add the water and stir. Leave
for about ten minutes or until some froth has formed on
the top. Sift the dry ingredients into a large bowl and
make a well in the centre. Add the yeast liquid and butter
and mix to a dough. Knead by hand (or using an electric
mixer with a dough hook) for seven to ten minutes.
Cover with greased or oiled cling film (plastic wrap) and
leave for about an hour to an hour and a quarter or until
double in size.

Punch down the dough and divide in half. Form into
two balls and place each in greased 500 g/1 lb loaf pans,
or shape into round loaves and slash tops with a sharp
knife. Cover again and leave for about an hour or until
double in size.

Beat the egg white with water and brush over the tops
of the loaves. Bake in a hot oven, 220°C/425°F, gas 7 for
five minutes. Reduce to moderate, 190°C/375°F, gas 5
and bake a further 20 to 25 minutes.

Black bread ▷

CRANBERRY RYE BREAD

Use the cranberry sauce that is widely available in cans or jars from supermarkets for this recipe. The slight fruity taste of the bread makes it an ideal partner for chicken, turkey, or any poultry dish.

Metric/Imperial	Ingredients	American
8 g/2 tsp	Dried (active dry) yeast	2 tsp
2 tsp	Honey	2 tsp
100 ml/3 fl oz	Warm milk	⅓ cup
250 g/8 oz	Strong white (all-purpose) flour	2 cups
250 g/8 oz	Rye flour	1¾ cups
1½ tsp	Salt	1½ tsp
200 ml/6 fl oz	Cranberry sauce, made with whole cranberries	scant ¾ cup
2 tsp	Grated lemon rind	2 tsp
	Glaze (optional)	
1 tbsp	Sugar	1 tbsp
2 tbsp	Water	2 tbsp

Place the yeast, honey and warm milk in a bowl and stir. Leave to stand for about ten minutes or until some froth has formed on top. Sift the flours and salt into a bowl. Warm the cranberry sauce and lemon rind until tepid. Make a well in the flour, add the yeast liquid and the cranberries and mix to a dough.

Knead by hand (or using an electric mixer with a dough hook) for seven to ten minutes. If too wet, add a little strong white (all-purpose) flour; if the mixture seems dry, moisten with some warm milk or warm water. It should be a slightly sticky dough as you begin; as it is kneaded it will become elastic and lose some moisture. Cover with greased or oiled cling film (plastic wrap) and leave in a warm place for about an hour until doubled. Punch down the dough and divide in half. Form each portion into a ball and place in a 750 g/1½ lb greased loaf pan. Cover again and leave for about 45 minutes to an hour until doubled.

Bake in a hot oven, 230°C/450°F, gas 8 for ten minutes, reduce to moderately hot, 190°C/375°F, gas 5 and bake a further 20 minutes.

You can glaze the loaf after baking if you wish, depending on what it is to be served with, as the glaze will add slightly to its sweetness. Heat a tablespoon sugar and two tablespoons water in a pan until the sugar has dissolved. Boil for a minute until syrupy. Brush over the loaf while it is still warm.

MALT AND FRUIT BREAD

Malt lends a special flavour and sticky quality to this sweet bread. Leave it for 24 hours before cutting, then slice and serve buttered for morning coffee or afternoon tea. It is also good toasted. Unlike most other breads, it can be stored, well wrapped, in the refrigerator for about three weeks.

Metric/Imperial	Ingredients	American
8 g/2 tsp	Dried (active dry) yeast	2 tsp
3 tbsp	Malt extract	3 tbsp
4 tbsp	Hot water	4 tbsp
250 g/8 oz	Strong white (all-purpose) flour	2 cups
250 g/8 oz	Rye flour	1¾ cups
1 tsp	Salt	1 tsp
250 ml/8 fl oz	Warm water	1 cup
90 g/3 oz	Seedless raisins	½ cup
90 g/3 oz	Currants	½ cup
	Glaze	
2 tbsp	Sugar	2 tbsp
2 tbsp	Water	2 tbsp

Place the yeast in a bowl. Mix the malt extract with the very hot water and stir so the malt becomes more liquid. Add to the yeast and stir. Leave to stand for about five minutes or until some froth has formed on top.

Sift the flours and the salt into a bowl. Make a well in the centre, add the yeast liquid and additional warm water. Mix to a dough. Knead by hand (or using an electric mixer with a dough hook) for seven to ten minutes. Add the raisins and currants and knead again by hand until they are mixed through. The dough will be very solid. Cover with greased or oiled cling film (plastic wrap) and leave to stand in a warm place for about an hour and a half until almost doubled.

Punch down and form into a loaf. Place in a greased 500 g/1 lb loaf pan. Cover again and leave to prove until almost doubled. As this is a sticky, dense dough, it takes longer to rise than the usual bread dough, so be patient.

Bake in a hot oven, 230°C/450°F, gas 8 for ten minutes. Reduce to 190°C/375°F, gas 5 and bake a further 20 to 25 minutes. If browning too much cover loosely on top with foil.

Warm the sugar and water for the glaze until the sugar has dissolved and the mixture is slightly syrupy. Brush over the top of the loaf while it is still warm.

Malt and fruit bread ▷

SWEET BUN BREAD

SWEET BUN BREAD

This recipe makes bread that is beautifully light, with a fine crumb and a soft texture. Though not as simple as the basic white and wholemeal (whole wheat) breads, it is not too complicated, even for a beginner.

Butter and eggs enrich the dough, which is soft and sticky; add a little extra flour if it is too wet, but not too much, or the finished bread will not be so light. The dough rises quickly as a larger quantity of sugar helps to activate the yeast. Some of the buns in this section, however, which have generous added quantities of butter and are very rich, will take longer to prove, as will those which include a large amount of dried fruit. It is best not to cook this type of sweet bun at too high a temperature for long, though sufficient heat is needed at the start of baking to kill the yeast. Too high a temperature will give a hard, brown crust more suitable for savoury breads, rather than the soft, spongy crust that is typical of sweet breads. Watch them carefully when baking, as the extra sugar will cause them to colour more quickly; cover with foil if they brown too soon.

Be creative with the basic mixture by adding spices, dried fruit or nuts. Shape the dough as you choose, or according to how the bread will be served – as iced buns, perhaps, or sliced and spread with soft cheese and fruit preserve.

Most sweet breads are best eaten the day they are made, although they can be reheated, wrapped in foil, in a moderate oven, 180°C/350°F, gas 4, for about ten minutes.

Metric/Imperial	Ingredients	American
16 g/4 tsp	Dried (active dry) yeast	4 tsp
3 tbsp	Sugar	3 tbsp
250 ml/8 fl oz	Warm water	1 cup
500 g/1 lb	Strong white (all-purpose) flour	4 cups
1 tsp	Salt	1 tsp
1 tbsp	Skim-milk powder	1 tbsp
30 g/1 oz	Butter or margarine	2 tbsp
1	Egg	1
125 g/4 oz	Seedless raisins	¾ cup
	Glaze	
4 tbsp	Sugar	4 tbsp
4 tbsp	Water	4 tbsp

Mix the yeast with the sugar and warm water in a small bowl and stir. Leave to stand for a couple of minutes or until some froth has formed on top. Sift the flour, salt and skim-milk powder into a bowl and rub in the butter. Add the egg to the yeast and beat with a fork. Make a well in the centre of the flour, add the yeast liquid and mix to a dough.

Knead by hand (or in an electric mixer using a dough hook) for seven to ten minutes. Add the raisins and mix through by hand. Cover with greased or oiled cling film (plastic wrap) and leave in a warm place for about an hour until doubled.

Punch down and either form into small buns, or round or oval free-form loaves. This quantity makes twenty small buns, two large round loaves or three oval loaves. Place the buns or loaves on a greased baking tray (cookie sheet), cover again and leave to rise for about 45 minutes until doubled.

Bake in a hot oven 230°C/450°F, gas 8 for five minutes, reduce to 190°C/375°F, gas 5 and bake a further five minutes if you have made individual buns. If you have made two free-form loaves bake a further 15 to 20 minutes. If the large loaves begin to brown too much as they bake, cover on top lightly with some foil.

When cooked, remove to a rack to cool and glaze while still warm. To make the glaze, boil the sugar and water until syrupy, then brush over the top of the buns or loaves.

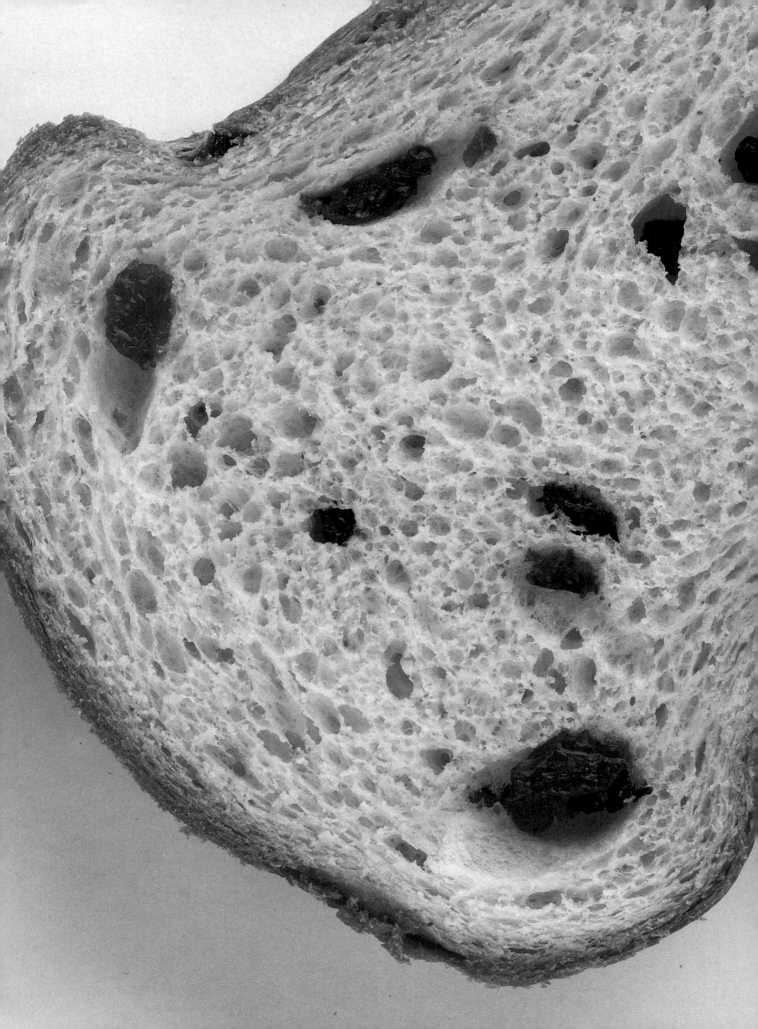

BRIOCHE

Brioche, a light yeast bread rich with butter and eggs, is eaten in France for breakfast, either warm from the oven or toasted and spread with butter and jam. It is also very good dunked into hot coffee!

Because of the high proportion of butter and eggs, brioche has a melt-in-the-mouth texture, much lighter and quite different from other yeast breads. It is not difficult to make, but do follow the directions carefully and note that it is best if allowed to rise very slowly in a gentle warmth.

An interesting way to serve this special bread is to hollow out the base and top and warm them in the oven without letting them become too crisp. Fill the base with creamed chicken, mushrooms or seafood, replace the top and serve cut in wedges like a cake. Or use stale brioche slices to make a bread and butter pudding with cream, eggs and some raisins soaked in brandy – much more sophisticated than the familiar nursery version.

Metric/Imperial	Ingredients	American
16 g/4 tsp	Dried (active dry) yeast	4 tsp
3 tbsp	Sugar	3 tbsp
4 tbsp	Warm water	4 tbsp
500 g/1 lb	Strong white (all-purpose) flour	4 cups
1 tsp	Salt	1 tsp
4	Large eggs	4
185 g/6 oz	Butter, at room temperature	¾ cup
	Glaze	
1	Egg	1
2 tsp	Water	2 tsp

Place the yeast with a teaspoon of the sugar in a bowl. Add the warm water and stir. Leave to stand for about ten minutes or until some froth has formed on top. Place the remaining sugar in a bowl. Sift the flour and salt over it, mix, and make a well in the centre. Beat the eggs with a fork, add them to the yeast and then tip this into the centre of the flour. Mix to a dough.

Cut the butter into small pieces. A little at a time add the pieces of butter, mixing them in well so they are gradually incorporated into the dough. You can mix the dough with your hands, but it is much quicker if you use an electric mixer and a dough hook. When it has all been added, the dough should be very moist, almost sticky and soft, but not so wet that it would not sit on the end of a spoon for a few seconds. The dough will be too soft to knead. Cover the bowl with greased or oiled cling film (plastic wrap) and place a cloth on top. Leave at room temperature for about an hour to an hour and a half or until it has doubled.

Place the dough in the refrigerator, still covered, and leave for about 12 hours to firm and become quite cold. It is best to leave it overnight. Next day punch down the dough. Take off a small piece, about a quarter, and form the larger piece into a round smooth ball by pulling the dough surface to the underside. Form the small piece into a ball and pull down some of the base to form a teardrop shape. It should be smooth on top. Grease a large brioche pan with a capacity of about 1.5 l/2¾ pints (7 cups).

Place the large ball of dough into the pan and make a hole in the centre with your fingers. Insert the smaller piece of dough with the tail end down into this. Push gently with your index finger between these two at intervals. Cover again and leave at room temperature, not in too warm a position. The more gently this rises the better. It should double in size and may take up to four hours.

When risen, beat the egg with water for the glaze and brush over the top and sides of the dough. Place in a hot oven, 220°C/425°F, gas 7 for 15 minutes, reduce the oven temperature to 190°C/375°F, gas 5 and bake a further 15 to 20 minutes.

Take the brioche out of the oven and leave in the pan for a couple of minutes; check it is loosened on all sides before turning out. Do not tip out onto a rack, or you may break the top knot. Cool with the base down and the little top section upwards. Store wrapped in foil. Reheat in foil in a moderate oven, 190°C/375°F, gas 5 for about 12 minutes.

Brioche ▷

CHERRY ALMOND WREATH

One of the prettiest of all the sweet breads, this has a festive appearance with bright pieces of cherry peeping through the layers, making it specially suitable to serve at Christmas or other holiday times. Red cherries are the easiest to buy, but a mixture of red, green and yellow could be used for a more colourful effect.

Metric/Imperial	Ingredients	American
12 g/3 tsp	Dried (active dry) yeast	3 tsp
3 tbsp	Caster (powdered) sugar	3 tbsp
250 ml/8 fl oz	Warm water	1 cup
400 g/13 oz	Strong white (all-purpose) flour	3 cups
¾ tsp	Salt	¾ tsp
30 g/1 oz	Butter or margarine	2 tbsp
	Filling	
60 g/2 oz	Unsalted (sweet) butter	4 tbsp
3 tbsp	Flour	3 tbsp
1 tbsp	Icing (confectioners') sugar	1 tbsp
185 g/6 oz	Glacé cherries, cut into small pieces	1 cup
90 g/3 oz	Slivered almonds	½ cup
2 tsp	Grated lemon rind	2 tsp
Few drops	Almond essence (extract)	Few drops
	Icing	
90 g/3 oz	Icing (confectioners') sugar	¾ cup
2 tsp	Lemon juice	2 tsp
	Water	

Place the yeast and sugar in a small bowl, add the warm water and stir. Leave to stand until some froth has formed on top. Sift the flour and salt into a bowl, add the butter and rub in. Make a well in the centre, add the yeast liquid and mix to a dough. Knead by hand (or using an electric mixer with a dough hook) for seven to ten minutes. Cover with greased or oiled cling film (plastic wrap) and leave in a warm place for about an hour until doubled.

Prepare the filling while the dough is rising. Mash the butter, flour and sugar with a fork. Add the cherries, almonds and lemon rind and flavour with almond essence (extract). Blend well.

Roll the dough out to form a rectangle about 30 x 23 cm/12 x 9 in. Dot the cherry mixture over the top, keeping it clear of the edges. Roll up lengthways like a Swiss roll (jelly roll). Continue to roll gently with your hands to make it even thinner and about twice as long. Cut lengthways into two strips, using a very sharp serrated knife so it will slice through the nuts. Twist these two pieces of dough around each other, keeping the cut sides upwards so the filling can be seen. Form a circle and place on a greased baking tray (cookie sheet). Cover again and leave in a warm place for about 45 minutes until almost doubled.

Place in a hot oven 220°C/425°F, gas 7 and bake for five minutes, reduce to 190°C/375°F, gas 5 and bake for another 20 minutes, covering the top with foil if it becomes too brown. Remove from the oven and leave to rest on the tray for five minutes before transferring to a wire rack.

Ice the wreath while it is still warm. Mix the sugar, lemon juice and water to a fairly thin consistency and trickle over the wreath in an uneven pattern.

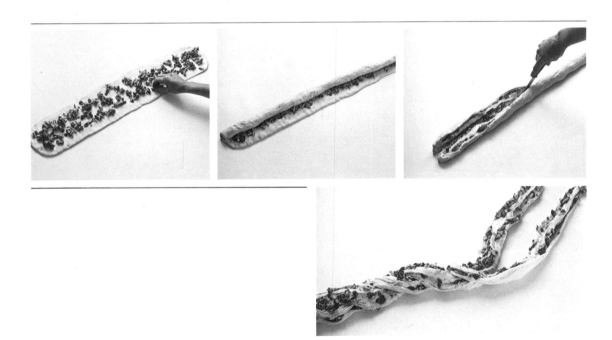

Cherry almond wreath ▷

CHOCOLATE CRESCENTS

These are great favourites with lovers of chocolate. Serve as a Sunday morning treat or at a leisurely weekend brunch. They reheat well, wrapped in foil, and can also be frozen.

Metric/Imperial	Ingredients	American
16 g/4 tsp	Dried (active dry) yeast	4 tsp
125 ml/4 fl oz	Warm water	½ cup
140 ml/5 fl oz	Warm milk	⅔ cup
500 g/1 lb	Strong white (all-purpose) flour	4 cups
¾ tsp	Salt	¾ tsp
2 tbsp	Sugar	2 tbsp
	Filling	
30 g/1 oz	Butter or margarine, melted	2 tbsp
1 tbsp	Sugar	1 tbsp
3 tbsp	Finely chopped hazelnuts	3 tbsp
60 g/2 oz	Dark (semisweet) chocolate, grated or finely chopped	8 tbsp

Place the yeast in a bowl, add the warm water and stir. Leave to stand for about ten minutes or until some froth has formed on top. Add the warm milk. Sift the flour, salt and sugar into a bowl. Make a well in the centre, add the yeast liquid and mix to a dough. Knead by hand (or using an electric mixer with a dough hook) for seven to ten minutes. Cover with greased or oiled cling film (plastic wrap) and leave to stand in a warm place for about an hour until doubled.

Punch down and divide in half. Roll each piece into a round ball, then roll out into a 30 cm/12 in circle.

Using a pastry brush, spread the dough with the melted butter. Mix the sugar and hazelnuts and scatter over the top. Sprinkle with grated chocolate. Using a sharp knife, cut each circle into eight wedges. Beginning at the wide end, roll up to form a crescent.

Place on greased baking trays (cookie sheets). Cover with a piece of greased or oiled cling film (plastic wrap). Leave to prove in a warm place until doubled.

Bake in a hot oven, 220°C/425°F, gas 7 for five minutes, reduce to 190°C/375°F, gas 5 and bake a further seven minutes. Makes 16 crescents.

CINNAMON AND WALNUT HORSESHOES

These tempting buns have a filling of butter, sugar, cinnamon and walnuts spread over the dough to form a sweet, spicy layer. Quick and simple to make, the dough is best formed into two small horseshoes rather than one large one. These are nicest eaten the day they are made, but can be reheated, wrapped in foil.

Metric/Imperial	Ingredients	American
16 g/4 tsp	Dried (active dry) yeast	4 tsp
3 tbsp	Sugar	3 tbsp
75 ml/3 fl oz	Warm water	⅓ cup
150 ml/5 fl oz	Warm milk	⅔ cup
30 g/1 oz	Unsalted (sweet) butter	2 tbsp
1	Egg, beaten	1
500 g/1 lb	Strong white (all-purpose) flour	4 cups
1 tsp	Salt	1 tsp
1 tsp	Cinnamon	1 tsp
60 g/2 oz	Unsalted (sweet) butter	4 tbsp
90 g/3 oz	Brown sugar	½ cup
90 g/3 oz	Chopped walnuts	¾ cup
	Glaze	
4 tbsp	Sugar	4 tbsp
3 tbsp	Water	3 tbsp
1 tsp	Instant coffee powder	1 tsp

Place the yeast, sugar and warm water in a small bowl and stir. Leave for about five minutes until some froth has formed on top. Have the milk warm and add the butter, cut into small pieces. Add the beaten egg to the yeast. Sift the flour and salt into a basin, make a well in the centre and add the yeast liquid and milk. Mix to a dough. If too sticky, add a little more flour as you knead, if too dry, a little warm water. It should be very moist.

Knead by hand (or use an electric mixer with a dough hook) for seven to ten minutes. Cover with greased or oiled cling film (plastic wrap) and leave in a warm place for about 45 minutes until doubled.

Mix the cinnamon, butter and sugar together until soft. Add the walnuts. Punch down the dough, divide in half and roll out to oblong shapes, about 20 x 15 cm/8 x 6 in. Dot the butter and sugar mixture over the top, but not right to the edges. Roll up like a Swiss roll (jelly roll), pinching the ends so the filling will not leak.

Place each roll on a baking tray (cookie sheet) and bend into a horseshoe shape. Cover with greased cling film (plastic wrap) and leave in a warm place for about 45 minutes until doubled.

Place in a hot oven, 220°C/425°F, gas 7 and bake for ten minutes. Reduce to 190°C/375°F, gas 5 and bake a further ten minutes. If becoming too brown, cover loosely with foil. Remove from the oven and leave to cool.

For the glaze, heat the sugar and water until the sugar has dissolved. Dissolve the instant coffee in a spoonful of water, add to the sugar and water and heat until slightly syrupy. Brush over the top of the horseshoes.

Chocolate crescents ▷

COFFEE SCROLLS

In spite of their name, these lightly spiced and fruited buns contain no coffee: the name merely indicates that they are ideal served with coffee, or tea.

Mix the dried fruit into the dough by hand after the initial kneading, even if you are using an electric mixer, and knead again thoroughly to incorporate it evenly. Divide the dough into sixteen portions, as suggested, or make larger or smaller buns if you prefer.

Metric/Imperial	Ingredients	American
8 g/2 tsp	Dried (active dry) yeast	2 tsp
2 tbsp	Sugar	2 tbsp
75 ml/3 fl oz	Warm milk	⅓ cup
250 g/8 oz	Strong white (all-purpose) flour	2 cups
½ tsp	Salt	½ tsp
½ tsp	Mixed spice (apple or pumpkin pie spice)	½ tsp
½ tsp	Nutmeg	½ tsp
30 g/1 oz	Butter	2 tbsp
1	Egg, beaten	1
60 g/2 oz	Sultanas (golden raisins)	⅓ cup
2 tbsp	Currants	2 tbsp
1 tbsp	Mixed (candied citrus) peel	1 tbsp
15 g/½ oz	Butter	1 tbsp
60 g/2 oz	Brown sugar	½ cup
1 tsp	Cinnamon	1 tsp
	Icing	
90 g/3 oz	Icing (confectioners') sugar	⅔ cup
	Warm water (see recipe)	

Place the yeast, sugar and warm milk in a bowl and stir. Leave to stand for a few minutes until some froth has formed on top. Sift the flour, salt, mixed (apple pie) spice and nutmeg into a large bowl. Rub the butter into the flour. Make a well in the centre, add the yeast liquid and egg and mix to a dough. Knead by hand (or using an electric mixer with a dough hook) for about five to seven minutes.

Add the dried fruit and peel and knead by hand to mix in evenly. Cover with greased or oiled cling film (plastic wrap) and leave in a warm place for about 45 minutes until doubled.

Punch down the dough and roll into a rectangle, about 40 x 25 cm/16 x 10 in. Melt the 15 g/½ oz/(1 tbsp) butter and brush on top. Mix the brown sugar and cinnamon together and scatter evenly over the dough. Roll up tightly like a Swiss roll (jelly roll). Cut into about 16 slices. Place well apart on a greased baking tray (cookie sheet) and press down firmly with your hand so they are slightly flattened; or arrange them so they are almost touching and will join when proved and baked. Cover again and leave for about 45 minutes until doubled.

Bake at 220°C/425°F, gas 7 for about eight minutes. If proved so the buns are touching each other, allow ten to 12 minutes. Ice while they are slightly warm.

Mix the icing (confectioners') sugar with sufficient warm water to make an icing which will spread easily. Place a little in the centre of each bun – it will spread out to cover the top.

Coffee scrolls ▷

92

FRUIT BRAID

This is a decorative bread, with the dough folded in a lattice pattern across a rich, fruity filling.

Serve it plain, in slices, to accompany tea or coffee, or more festively with whipped cream or ice cream. It can be reheated in a moderate oven, 180°C/350°F, gas 4, covered lightly with foil.

Metric/Imperial	Ingredients	American
500 g/1 lb	Pears or cooking apples	1 lb
4 tbsp	Sugar	4 tbsp
3 tsp	Grated orange rind	3 tsp
125 ml/4 fl oz	Orange juice	½ cup
250 g/8 oz	Seedless raisins	1½ cups
1 tbsp	Chopped stem (candied) ginger	1 tbsp
3 tbsp	Finely chopped dried apricots	3 tbsp
	Dough	
12 g/3 tsp	Dried (active dry) yeast	3 tsp
2 tbsp	Sugar	2 tbsp
200 ml/6 fl oz	Warm water	¾ cup
400 g/13 oz	Strong white (all-purpose) flour	3 cups
¾ tsp	Salt	¾ tsp
2 tsp	Skim-milk powder	2 tsp
30 g/1 oz	Butter or margarine	2 tbsp
1	Egg, beaten	1
	Glaze	
3 tbsp	Orange juice	3 tbsp
3 tbsp	Sugar	3 tbsp

Prepare the filling first. It can be made the day before, but should be removed from the refrigerator an hour before using, so that it is not too cold.

Peel and core the pears or apples, and cut them into small dice. Place in a saucepan with the sugar, orange rind and juice. Cook gently for about five minutes. Add the raisins, chopped ginger and apricots and cook without a lid over low heat until the fruit is tender.

If any liquid has formed, turn up the heat and boil for a few minutes, but make sure the fruit does not burn. Cool in a basin.

Place the yeast, sugar and warm water in a basin and stir. Leave to stand for five minutes or until some froth has formed on top. Sift the flour, salt and skim-milk powder into a basin and rub in the butter. Make a well in the centre, add the yeast liquid and beaten egg. Mix to a dough; it should be very moist. Knead by hand (or in an electric mixer using a dough hook) for seven to ten minutes. Cover with greased or oiled cling film (plastic wrap) and leave in a warm place for about 45 minutes to an hour until doubled.

Roll out the dough to an oblong shape, about 35 × 23 cm/14 × 9 in. Before filling with fruit, place on a large greased baking tray (cookie sheet), as it is impossible to move in one piece once filled. Place the fruit in a strip down the centre. Cut each side of the dough with a sharp knife or scissors into fourteen strips. Make sure you have an equal number on both sides. Turn the end over, then plait the strips, turning up at the base. The fruit should show slightly through the lattice.

Cover again and leave in a warm place until risen, but do not let this quite double or it will be too thick.

Bake in a hot oven, 220°C/425°F, gas 7 for five minutes. Reduce to moderate, 180°C/350°F, gas 4 and bake a further 20 minutes. Remove from the oven and glaze when slightly cool.

Place the orange juice and sugar in a small saucepan and cook until the sugar has dissolved and the mixture is slightly syrupy. Brush over the top of the braid.

Fruit braid ▷

APRICOT STREUSEL SLICE

In this recipe, fruits – which could be apricots, peaches, plums or apples – sit on a light bread base, and are topped with a rich, crunchy streusel, a crumbly mixture of butter, sugar, flour and coconut.

The slice may appear a little wet in the centre when it comes out of the oven, so check that the crust is cooked. As it cools and the juices settle, it will firm up in the centre. It keeps well for several days and can be reheated before eating. Serve warm with cream, ice cream or vanilla custard. The quantity serves ten or more.

Metric/Imperial	Ingredients	American
12 g/3 tsp	Dried (active dry) yeast	3 tsp
3 tbsp	Sugar	3 tbsp
250 ml/8 fl oz	Warm water	1 cup
30 g/1 oz	Butter, melted	2 tbsp
400 g/13 oz	Strong white (all-purpose) flour	3 cups
1 tsp	Salt	1 tsp
825 g/1 lb 11 oz	Canned apricots	3½ cups
125 g/4 oz	Apricot jam	½ cup
2 tbsp	Lemon or orange juice	2 tbsp
	Streusel topping	
185 g/6 oz	Caster (powdered) sugar	1 cup
90 g/3 oz	Unsalted (sweet) butter, melted	6 tbsp
60 g/2 oz	Flour	½ cup
45 g/1½ oz	Desiccated (dried, shredded) coconut	½ cup

Place the yeast, sugar and warm water in a small bowl and stir. Leave for about five minutes or until some froth has formed on top. Add the melted butter. Sift the flour and salt into a large bowl. Make a well in the centre, add the yeast liquid and mix to a dough. Knead by hand (or in an electric mixer using a dough hook) for seven to ten minutes. Cover with greased or oiled cling film (plastic wrap) and leave to stand in a warm place for about an hour until doubled in size.

Drain the apricots and pat dry on kitchen paper.

Punch down the dough and roll out so it is large enough to fit into a greased baking dish with shallow sides, about 30 x 23 cm/12 x 9 in. Press gently on the edges to make a shallow casing. Cover again and leave to rise about ten minutes. It should puff slightly, but do not let it rise too much or the crust will be too thick.

Warm the jam with the juice and spread over the dough. Arrange the apricot halves on top, cut side down. Mix the streusel ingredients together and scatter over the top.

Bake in a hot oven, 220°C/425°F, gas 7 for ten minutes. Reduce to moderate, 190°C/375°F, gas 5 and bake a further 30 minutes or until the topping is golden.

APPLE STREUSEL SLICE

Prepare the dough as for Apricot Streusel Slice.

Metric/Imperial	Ingredients	American
125 g/4 oz	Apricot jam	½ cup
2 tbsp	Lemon or orange juice	2 tbsp
825 g/1 lb 11 oz	Canned apples, sliced	3½ cups
	Streusel topping	
90 g/3 oz	Light brown sugar	½ cup
90 g/3 oz	Butter, melted	6 tbsp
60 g/2 oz	Flour	½ cup
1 tsp	Cinnamon	1 tsp
45 g/1½ oz	Desiccated (dried, shredded) coconut	½ cup

Warm the apricot jam and fruit juice and spread over the dough. Top with the drained apples, spreading them evenly. Mix the streusel ingredients and scatter over the apple. Bake as for Apricot Streusel Slice.

PLUM STREUSEL SLICE

Prepare the dough as for Apricot Streusel Slice.

Use either 125 g/4 oz (½ cup) redcurrant jelly or plum jam, warmed and spread on the base. Drain very well 825 g/1 lb 11 oz (3½ cups) of canned plums. Cut in half and remove stones. Place the plums cut side down on the dough and scatter the streusel mixture on top. Bake as above.

Fruit streusel slice ▷

MONKEY BREAD

It is difficult to imagine how the curious name of this bread originated. Nevertheless it is delicious, and a special treat for children of all ages.

The tiny sections of dough are dipped into a mixture of sugar and butter before baking, which forms a caramel-flavoured coating on each piece.

Eat this fresh and warm from the oven, or reheat it the next day.

Metric/Imperial	Ingredients	American
16 g/4 tsp	Dried (active dry) yeast	4 tsp
3 tbsp	Sugar	3 tbsp
200 ml/6 fl oz	Warm milk	¾ cup
60 g/2 oz	Unsalted (sweet) butter, cut into small pieces	4 tbsp
1	Egg	1
500 g/1 lb	Strong white (all-purpose) flour	4 cups
1 tsp	Salt	1 tsp
1 tsp	Cinnamon	1 tsp
90 g/3 oz	Seedless raisins	½ cup
125 g/4 oz	Unsalted (sweet) butter	½ cup
90 g/3 oz	Light brown sugar	½ cup

Place the yeast, sugar and about half the milk in a small bowl and stir. Leave to stand for five minutes or until some froth has formed on top. Add the pieces of butter to the remaining warm milk. The butter should melt, but if any small pieces remain this does not matter.

Beat the egg and add to the milk. Mix into the yeast. Sift the flour, salt and cinnamon. Make a well in the centre, add the yeast liquid and mix to a dough. It should be very moist. Knead by hand (or in an electric mixer using a dough hook) for seven to ten minutes. Add the raisins and knead these in by hand until evenly distributed through the mixture.

Cover with greased or oiled cling film (plastic wrap) and leave in a warm place for about 45 minutes to an hour until doubled. Divide the dough into about forty small balls, each about the size of a walnut.

Melt the 125 g/4 oz (½ cup) butter in a saucepan, add the brown sugar and stir well to mix. Use a well-greased angel cake tube pan for this bread or a large cake pan with a central hole. It should be about 3 1/5 pints (12 cups) capacity, or use two smaller ones.

Dip the balls into the butter and sugar, and place them evenly around the bottom of the pan. Continue building up the layers, stirring the butter and sugar mixture occasionally if the sugar sinks to the bottom of the pan. Pour any remaining syrup over the top of the balls. They should come about halfway up the pan. Cover again and leave for about 45 minutes until doubled.

Bake in a hot oven, 220°C/425°F, gas 7 for 15 minutes. Reduce to 180°C/350°F, gas 4 and bake a further 15 minutes. Cover the top loosely with foil so the bread will not brown too much. When cooked, loosen around the edge of the pan with a knife but do not turn out immediately; leave for ten minutes. Turn out onto a cake rack, but leave the pan resting on top until almost cool; this will prevent the balls separating.

Pull away the little sections of bun to serve at the table. To reheat, wrap in foil and place in a moderate oven, 180°C/350°F, gas 4 for about 12 to 15 minutes.

Monkey bread ▷

SIMPLE FRUIT LOAF

Simple to make, with a lovely flavour and texture, this loaf can be eaten buttered when fresh, or toasted when a day or more old.

Metric/Imperial	Ingredients	American
16 g/4 tsp	Dried (active dry) yeast	4 tsp
3 tbsp	Sugar	3 tbsp
150 ml/5 fl oz	Warm water	⅔ cup
100 ml/3 fl oz	Warm milk	⅓ cup
30 g/1 oz	Butter or margarine, melted	2 tbsp
1	Egg, beaten	1
500 g/1 lb	Strong white (all-purpose) flour	4 cups
1 tsp	Salt	1 tsp
1 tsp	Mixed spice (apple or pumpkin pie spice)	1 tsp
2 tsp	Cinnamon	2 tsp
185 g/6 oz	Seedless raisins	1 cup
90 g/3 oz	Currants	½ cup
	Glaze	
2 tbsp	Water	2 tbsp
2 tbsp	Sugar	2 tbsp

Place the yeast, sugar and warm water in a bowl and stir. Leave to stand for five minutes or until some froth has formed on top. Add the warm milk, butter or margarine and egg. Sift the flour, salt and spices into a bowl. Make a well in the centre, add the yeast liquid and mix to a dough. Knead by hand (or in an electric mixer using a dough hook) for seven to ten minutes. Add the raisins and currants and knead by hand until they are mixed in evenly. Cover with greased or oiled cling film (plastic wrap) and leave in a warm place for about 45 minutes to an hour until doubled.

Punch down and shape into two balls. Place in a 750 g/1½ lb greased loaf pan and cover again. Leave in a warm place for about 45 minutes until doubled.

Bake in a hot oven, 220°C/425°F, gas 7 for 15 minutes. Reduce to 190°C/375°F, gas 5 and bake a further ten to 15 minutes. If becoming too brown on top, cover loosely with foil. Glaze while slightly warm.

For the glaze, heat the water and sugar until the sugar has dissolved and the mixture is slightly syrupy. Brush over the top of the loaf.

SPECIAL CHOCOLATE ORANGE BUNS

In these delicious buns, a subtly orange-flavoured crust encases a generous amount of melted chocolate. Wonderful for brunch or as a snack, they can be frozen and reheated after thawing.

Metric/Imperial	Ingredients	American
16 g/4 tsp	Dried (active dry) yeast	4 tsp
125 ml/4 fl oz	Warm water	½ cup
140 ml/6 fl oz	Warm milk	⅔ cup
3 tsp	Grated orange rind	3 tsp
500 g/1 lb	Strong white (all-purpose) flour	4 cups
¾ tsp	Salt	¾ tsp
2 tbsp	Sugar	2 tbsp
250 g/8 oz	Dark (semisweet) grated chocolate or chocolate chips	½ lb
	Glaze	
2 tbsp	Water	2 tbsp
2 tbsp	Sugar	2 tbsp

Place the yeast in a bowl, add the warm water and stir. Leave to stand for about ten minutes or until some froth has formed on top. Add the warm milk and grated orange rind.

Sift the flour, salt and sugar into a bowl. Make a well in the centre. Add the yeast liquid and mix to a dough. Knead by hand (or using an electric mixer with a dough hook) for seven to ten minutes. Cover the dough with greased or oiled cling film (plastic wrap) and leave for about an hour until doubled.

Punch down the dough and divide into 18 pieces. With a rolling pin, flatten them out to an oblong shape; they should be quite thin. Place about one tablespoon of the chocolate chips or grated chocolate down the centre of each piece of dough, taking the strip close to each end so every bite will have chocolate in the centre. Roll over to enclose, tucking the ends in. Be sure that the chocolate does not come through. Pinch well to join the seams.

Place the buns on a lightly greased baking tray (cookie sheet), join side down. Cover and leave in a warm place until doubled.

Bake in a hot oven, 220°C/425°F, gas 7 for about 13 to 15 minutes. Cool slightly before glazing.

For the glaze, mix the water and sugar in a small pan and cook until the sugar has dissolved. Boil for two minutes and brush over the top of the buns. Leave for a few minutes before eating, as the chocolate remains quite hot.

To reheat, wrap in foil and place in a moderate oven, 180°C/350°F, gas 4 for about ten minutes.

Special chocolate orange buns ▷

STOLLEN

This rich, sweet bread is popular in Germany where it is served at Christmas. It is studded with nuts and a generous amount of fruit which is first soaked in brandy, rum or orange juice.

Although sweet, it is a rather dry, firm loaf which keeps well and is best served cut into very thin slices. Traditionally it is formed into an oblong for baking and then dusted with icing (confectioners') sugar. When stale it is excellent toasted.

Metric/Imperial	Ingredients	American
90 g/3 oz	Glacé cherries, quartered	½ cup
60 g/2 oz	Currants	½ cup
60 g/2 oz	Mixed (candied citrus) peel	½ cup
90 g/3 oz	Seedless raisins	½ cup
125 ml/4 fl oz	Orange juice, cognac or dark rum	½ cup
45 g/1½ oz	Slivered almonds	⅓ cup
16 g/4 tsp	Dried (active dry) yeast	4 tsp
½ tsp	Sugar	½ tsp
3 tbsp	Warm water	3 tbsp
75 ml/3 fl oz	Milk	½ cup
90 g/3 oz	Unsalted (sweet) butter	6 tbsp
2	Large eggs	2
500 g/1 lb	Strong white (all-purpose) flour	4 cups
1 tsp	Salt	1 tsp
2 tsp	Grated lemon rind	2 tsp
	Sifted icing (confectioners') sugar	

Place all the fruit in a bowl. Add the juice, cognac or rum and leave to soak for 12 hours or overnight. Strain and reserve any liquid. Mix the nuts into the fruit.

Place the yeast, sugar and warm water in a bowl and stir. Leave to stand for about ten minutes or until some froth has formed on top. Warm the milk in a saucepan until tepid. Cut the butter into small pieces and add off the heat. Leave until melted.

Beat the eggs, add to the milk and mix this into the yeast liquid. Sift the flour and salt into a bowl, add the lemon rind, and make a well in the centre. Add the liquid to the flour and mix to a dough. Knead by hand (or in an electric mixer using a dough hook) for seven to ten minutes. Add the fruit and nut mixture and reserved liquid and mix in by hand. If it becomes sticky, knead in a little flour. The dough should be moist, but hold a shape.

Cover with greased or oiled cling film (plastic wrap) and leave in a warm place until doubled. This is slow to rise and may take two hours.

Punch down the dough and form into an oblong, then flatten to an oval, about 23 x 30 cm/9 x 12 in and fold to make a half-moon shape. Press down lightly and form into a crescent. Place on a greased flat baking tray (cookie sheet) and cover again. Leave in a warm place for an hour and a half until almost doubled.

Bake in a hot oven, 220°C/425°F, gas 7 for about eight minutes, reduce to 190°C/375°F, gas 5 and bake a further 25 minutes. Remove and cool. Sift icing (confectioners') sugar over the top to form a frosted layer.

VERY RICH FRUIT LOAF

This is a wonderful loaf, fragrant with orange, spices and fruit. Eat it when fresh, simply buttered, or cut it into thin slices and toast them for a special breakfast treat or for morning or afternoon tea.

Closely wrapped and refrigerated, it will keep for up to ten days.

Metric/Imperial	Ingredients	American
16 g/4 tsp	Dried (active dry) yeast	4 tsp
125 ml/3 fl oz	Warm water	½ cup
75 ml/2 fl oz	Warm milk	¼ cup
185 g/6 oz	Seedless raisins	1 cup
90 g/3 oz	purrants	½ cup
90 g/3 oz	Mixed (candied citrus) peel	½ cup
3 tsp	Grated orange rind	3 tsp
500 g/1 lb	Strong white (all-purpose) flour	4 cups
3 tbsp	Sugar	3 tbsp
1 tsp	Salt	1 tsp
1 tsp	Nutmeg	1 tsp
2 tsp	Cinnamon	2 tsp
1	Egg, beaten	1
	Glaze	
2 tbsp	Sugar	2 tbsp
1 tbsp	Water	1 tbsp

Place the yeast in a bowl with the warm water and milk and stir. Leave to stand for about ten minutes or until some froth has formed on top. Mix the raisins and currants in another bowl. Pour boiling water over the top and leave for five minutes, then drain well. Mix with the peel and grated orange rind.

Sift the flour into a bowl with the sugar, salt, nutmeg and cinnamon and make a well in the centre. Stir in the yeast liquid, add the egg and mix to a dough. Knead by hand (or use an electric mixer with a dough hook) for seven to ten minutes. Add the fruit to the dough, kneading it in well. This is best done by hand. Cover with greased or oiled cling film (plastic wrap) and leave to rise for about an hour to an hour and a quarter or until doubled.

Punch the dough down, divide in half and form into two balls. Place in 500 g/1 lb greased loaf pans and cover. Leave to rise for about an hour or until doubled.

Place in a hot oven, 220°C/425°F, gas 7 and bake for 15 minutes. Reduce to moderately hot, 190°C/375°F, gas 5 and bake a further 15 minutes. Glaze the top while the loaf is still warm.

Heat the sugar and water together until the sugar has dissolved and the mixture is syrupy. Brush over the top of the loaf.

Very rich fruit loaf ▷

USES FOR STALE BREAD

The most obvious way to use up any leftover stale bread is by making breadcrumbs – for use as toppings on casseroles and mornay dishes to give a crisp coating, as well as for stuffings, and for coating pieces of meat or poultry before frying.

Breadcrumbs can be made using the crust as well as the inside of a loaf, either in a food processor, a coffee grinder or a coarse grater. They will keep for about ten days in a refrigerator, and for several months in the freezer.

As the crumbs dry out in the refrigerator, they become even more successful as a coating on dishes; there is no need to dry them in the oven. The cooking process will toast and brown them in any case.

BREAD ROLL CASES

Small bread rolls which are a few days old make the most successful cases and can be filled with many cooked savoury fillings, for example, mushrooms in a lightly thickened sauce; chicken or ham, diced small, in a creamy white or cheese sauce; oysters, fish or seafood or a selection of vegetables.

The only rules to follow are that the filling should be cooked, very tasty and just thick enough to bind well, but not so heavy that it will be too solid inside the bread.

The bread cases and filling can be prepared separately during the day, and then combined at dinner time and the filled rolls placed in the oven to heat. They take about ten minutes depending on size: the bread should be crisp and the filling piping hot right through.

Use small round rolls or individual long dinner rolls – white or brown are equally good. They can be served as a first course, for lunch or for dinner with salads.

Metric/Imperial	Ingredients	American
6	Small bread rolls	6
60 g/2 oz	Butter or margarine	4 tbsp
3 tbsp	Finely chopped parsley	3 tbsp
½ tsp	Mixed dried herbs	½ tsp

Cut the tops from the rolls, removing about one third. Scoop out the dry crumb, leaving only a thin layer on the inside of the crust. Melt the butter and, using a pastry brush, brush over the inside and outside of the cases. Mix the parsley and herbs and press a little of this inside the cases, on the edges and outside, to make a light scattering of green.

Place the rolls on a baking tray (cookie sheet) in a moderate oven, 190°C/375°F, gas 5 and bake for about five minutes or until slightly crisp. Do not overcook at this stage.

Fill when required and bake in a moderate oven, 190°C/375°F, gas 5 for about ten to 15 minutes, depending on the size of the rolls. Serve as soon as they are ready.

MELBA TOAST

The great chef Escoffier created this light toast for the famous singer Dame Nellie Melba. Thin and crunchy, this toast can be stored in an airtight tin for a week. Serve with pâté as a first course, or with soups. Use stale bread, preferably from the basic white or an enriched milk loaf.

Cut the crusts from thin slices of bread, trim the slices into squares and cut in half diagonally to make triangles.

Place on an ungreased baking tray (cookie sheet). Bake in a moderate oven, 180°C/350°F, gas 4 for about 15 minutes. Watch them carefully, as the timing will depend on the thickness and also how stale the bread was. They should be a golden colour and need turning over once or twice as they cook. The pieces will curl as they dry out. Leave to cool and then store in an airtight container.

Bread roll cases, Melba toast ▷